Ernest Hemingway
Complete Poems

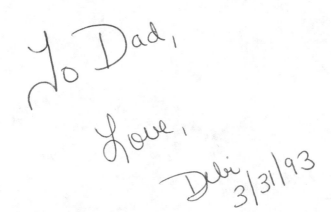

To Dad,

Love,

Debi 3/31/93

READ AGAIN 8-20-93
EN ROUTE PARIS — TAMPA —
VIA CINCINNATI —

Again 4/20/97 /20/93

Utah visit

Ernest

Complete Poems

Edited, with an introduction and Notes
by Nicholas Gerogiannis

Revised Edition

University of Nebraska Press

Lincoln and London

Hemingway

First Bison Book printing: February 1983

Revised Edition, 1992
Most recent printing of the Revised Edition indicated by the last digit below:
10   9   8   7   6   5   4   3   2

Library of Congress Cataloging-in-Publication Data
Hemingway, Ernest, 1899–1961.
[Poems]
Complete poems / edited with an introduction and notes by Nicholas
Gerogiannis.—Rev. ed.
p.   cm.
Rev. ed. of: 88 poems. 1979.
Includes bibliographical references.
ISBN 0-8032-7259-6 (pa)
I. Hemingway, Ernest, 1899–1961.   88 poems.   II. Title.
PS3515.E37A17   1992
811'.52—dc20
91-41862   CIP

Originally published as *Ernest Hemingway: 88 Poems*
Published by arrangement with Harcourt Brace Jovanovich, Inc.

∞

Contents

A Valentine and Other Offerings   1926-1935

Farewells 1944-1956

Introduction

In January 1923, *Poetry: A Magazine of Verse*[1] published six poems under the general title "Wanderings." Harriet Monroe, the editor, identified the author as "a young Chicago poet now abroad who will soon issue in Paris his first book of verse." Probably in August of that year, Robert McAlmon's Contact Publishing Company brought out *Three Stories & Ten Poems*—Ernest Hemingway's first book.

Hemingway never set out to become a poet, but like many other novelists—Joyce, Faulkner, and Fitzgerald, among others—he composed a certain amount of verse while he was becoming an established fiction writer. However, he continued to experiment with poetry after he had achieved literary fame. Discounting juvenilia, Hemingway published only twenty-five poems during his lifetime, but he was more productive as a poet than is commonly known. Of the eighty-eight[2] poems in this volume, seventy-three were completed by 1929 when *A Farewell to Arms* was published.

The "young Chicago poet" faded when the international author emerged, and since then the public's interest has been devoted to Hemingway the myth and Hemingway the fiction writer. Hemingway the poet is a contradictory figure—irascible and profane; a wit whose sense of humor was probably best appreciated by himself; a man outside of his generation, yet a writer for his time; and, in his middle and late years, a lonely man whose vigorous life of action was gradually overwhelmed by his memories, his illnesses, and his despair. In these poems a real man, not a myth, takes shape. Like the cumulative effect of sketches in an artist's notebook, the poems reveal Hemingway himself, rather than a fictional counterpart.

As a young man Hemingway attempted to work with many literary forms, often extending the techniques and styles that he had begun using while he was writing for the *Trapeze*, the Oak Park and River Forest High School newspaper, and the *Tabula*, the school's excellent literary magazine. Some of these early attempts echo the works of his first literary heroes, Rudyard Kipling and Ring Lardner, and strains from Carl Sandburg appear occasionally. Others show signs of a precocious talent that found it easy to parody the rhymes of Joyce Kilmer, James Whitcomb Riley, Robert Louis Stevenson, and even Robert Graves, among others. But Hemingway was a serious writer; it wasn't long before he became serious about his poetry.

Early signs of development appear with the poems that he wrote in Chicago in 1920 and 1921 (some of which he may have tried to publish). This first concerted effort at writing produced romantic and lyrical pieces that were affected by his memories of the war and his new love for Hadley Richardson. With his estrangement from his family nearly complete, he went to live with his friends the Y. K. Smiths in Chicago. He had been back from the war for over a year, and the time had come for him to begin putting into words what he had seen and felt. Some of the war poems that later appeared in *Poetry*, and were included in *Three Stories & Ten Poems*, were written during this time. The style that would later distinguish *In Our Time* was already in evidence in these short, quick attempts at giving the war artistic definition. He was also interested in the world around him. He saw clearly the lives of the men and women who inhabited the city, and in a few lines we have a rare glimpse of Hemingway as a socially conscious urban writer. But his inspiration—whether the subject was war, or love, or the city—was Hadley.

Hemingway arrived in Paris in December 1921. Four months later he met Gertrude Stein, and in a short time he became her disciple. Years later, in her self-portrait, *The Autobiography of Alice B. Toklas* (1933), Miss Stein wrote of Hemingway:

> He sat in front of Gertrude Stein and listened and looked.

They talked then, and more and more, a great deal together. He asked her to come and spend an evening in their apartment and look at his work. . . . We spent the evening there and he and Gertrude Stein went over all the writing he had done up to that time. He had begun the novel[3] that it was inevitable he would begin and there were the little poems afterwards printed by McAlmon in the Contact Edition. Gertrude Stein rather liked the poems, they were direct, Kiplingesque, but the novel she found wanting. There is a great deal of description in this, she said, and not particularly good description. <u>Begin over again and concentrate, she said.</u>[4]

[handwritten marginal note: "THE THREE DAY BLOW"]

[handwritten note: "THE SUN ALSO RISES" WAS WRITTEN IN PARIS]

Gertrude Stein felt that although Hemingway showed considerable talent, he did not yet understand the difficulty of writing well. She reinforced his sense of craftsmanship and artistic discipline. Whatever may have affected Hemingway's writing before he went to Paris, it is apparent that after he met Gertrude Stein her theories and works were strong influences on the poetry that he wrote. In "They All Made Peace—What Is Peace?" (1922) and "The Soul of Spain with McAlmon and Bird the Publishers" (1923) he used her distinctive style to satirize politicians and publishing. But their relationship could not last. In "Portrait of a Lady" (ca. 1926) Hemingway wrote a farewell to his former instructor in an echo of her own voice.

Another Paris mentor, Ezra Pound, not only influenced Hemingway's writing but made several spirited attempts to get his poems published. Pound's own phrase, "The age demanded,"[5] served Hemingway in one of his strongest poems. "He's teaching me to write," Hemingway wrote a friend, "and I'm teaching him to box."[6] As a founder of the Imagist movement, Pound liked the precise language and the carefully selected visual impressions in some of Hemingway's poems. When Ford Madox Ford needed an assistant editor for the *transatlantic review*, Pound recommended Hemingway. "He writes very good verse," he told Ford, "and he's the finest prose stylist in the world."[7] Pound thought well enough of

Hemingway's poetry to include it in magazines and anthologies that he edited.

Reflecting his associations with Stein and Pound, the poems that Hemingway wrote in Paris during the 1920s served as stylistic exercises and as vehicles for quick satire. As a young writer he had sought to liberate himself from several kinds of restrictions. He found models to help him: Kipling and Lardner offered escape from the boredom of Midwestern culture in Oak Park; the colorful journalists at the *Kansas City Star* helped free him from the constraining influences of his imposing mother and silent father; Gertrude Stein led him away from his early literary influences; and Ezra Pound helped correct his literary naiveté. The poems that Hemingway wrote are incidental to these influences, but they often dramatize his changing interests. They are markers in the most exciting and important period of his life. Sometimes they played minor roles in his attempts to establish himself as a writer.

Three Stories & Ten Poems was a surprise beginning to Hemingway's career. Ezra Pound had accepted *in our time*, a collection of prose vignettes, for a series of books that William Bird was publishing in Paris. This book was supposed to appear before *Three Stories & Ten Poems*, but Bird's Three Mountains Press worked slowly. As a result, by August of 1923 Robert McAlmon's Contact Publishing Company published Hemingway's first book. If it had not been for the poems, the book never would have been published. Eight months earlier, in December 1922, most of Hemingway's manuscripts had been lost when a valise that Hadley was carrying to Lausanne was stolen from her train compartment at the Gare de Lyon.[8] When McAlmon invited Hemingway to submit his material for publication, all that remained of his work were two stories, "Up In Michigan" and "My Old Man," and an assortment of poems. Later that spring, he completed "Out of Season" (a disturbing story that marks the true beginning of his mature style). Hemingway gave McAlmon these three stories, the six poems that had appeared in *Poetry* in January of that year, and four additional poems. It made a slim book, but it was nearly all he had.

Three hundred copies of *Three Stories & Ten Poems* were published, and it became a successful book in the Contact Editions series. Sylvia Beach sold copies at her bookstore, Shakespeare and Company, and Hemingway distributed copies by carrying them around Paris. He inscribed a copy to Gertrude Stein and Alice B. Toklas "with love from Hemingway."[9]

Although his early poetry was clearly apprentice work, Hemingway acknowledged its importance to the beginning of his career. In 1951 he wrote Charles A. Fenton: "The only work of mine that I endorse or sign as my true work is what I have published since *Three Stories & Ten Poems* and the first *In Our Time*."[10] These were thin volumes, a fact which he brooded over, but he was understandably proud. "I am glad to have it out," he wrote to Edmund Wilson a few months after *Three Stories & Ten Poems* appeared, "and once it is published it is back of you."[11]

The book was not widely reviewed, but initial critical reaction to Hemingway's poetry has been the standard one. In his review of *Three Stories & Ten Poems*, Wilson wrote: "Mr. Hemingway's poems are not particularly important, but his prose is of the first distinction."[12] After that, little more was said about the poems. Burton Rascoe, a literary columnist for the *New York Tribune*, finally "reviewed" *Three Stories & Ten Poems*—three months after Edmund Wilson had sent him a copy. But he only mentioned the title and added that he had not gotten around to reading the embarrassingly slim book.[13] Ford Madox Ford's *transatlantic review*, the journal that Hemingway had worked for, reviewed the book but ignored the ten poems altogether. Gertrude Stein wrote a review, which was published in the European edition of the *Chicago Tribune* (27 November 1923). The dismissal of his poems was an indication to Hemingway that they had served their purpose—as fillers for his first book. From then on he wrote only satirical verse for little magazines and a personal brand of poetry that was not meant for publication at all.

Ironically, after Hemingway gave up journalism in 1924 and returned to Paris from Toronto, he discovered that he was an American fiction writer who could sell poetry mostly to a German magazine. In continental Europe during the 1920s, *Der Querschnitt* (The Cross-Section) published an assortment of the best esoteric and avant-garde literature, along with some of the finest artwork to appear in any publication during this period. All prose that appeared in the magazine was in German, including Hemingway's long story, "The Undefeated." But the editors also published poems in English and French.

It was through a series of relationships that Hemingway's work began to appear in *Der Querschnitt*. At Shakespeare and Company, George Antheil, a young American composer living in Paris, met Count Alfred von Wedderkop, the Paris representative for the Frankfurt-based magazine. Count von Wedderkop, whose command of English was built around the phrase "awfully nice," thought that Antheil was a literary man and asked him to serve as Paris contributing editor to the magazine. Antheil, who was an enterprising sort, accepted the offer because he needed money. With friends like Sylvia Beach, Ford Madox Ford, and Ezra Pound, he knew where he could go for the needed material. One of the first authors whose work Antheil scouted for *Der Querschnitt* was James Joyce; selections from his volume of poetry, *Chamber Music*, were published in October 1923. Through Sylvia Beach and Ezra Pound, Antheil procured five poems from Hemingway; the first two were published in the autumn of 1924.[14] These poems received some attention. Eugene Jolas warned in "Open Letter to Ernest Hemingway" that the young author was much admired, but that Hemingway was on the wrong tack with the poems that he was publishing in *Der Querschnitt*.[15] Hemingway wrote in *A Moveable Feast* (1964) that he did not regard his German publications as significant, but that he needed the payments he received for his contributions to *Der Querschnitt*.

Hemingway rarely mentioned his poetry in his prose works. However, in *Green Hills of Africa* (1935), his nonfiction novel about a 1933 safari, he wrote of an encounter with an Austrian named Kandisky, a fictionalized name for Hans Koritschoner, who had an interest in contemporary literature. Hemingway introduced himself and Kandisky pondered the name:

> "Hemingway is a name I have heard. Where? Where have I heard it? Oh, yes. The *dichter*. You know Hemingway the Poet?"
>   "Where did you read him?"
>   "In the *Querschnitt*."
>   "That is me," I said, very pleased. The *Querschnitt* was a German magazine I had written some rather obscene poems for, and published a long story in, years before I could sell anything in America.[16]

Kandisky then drew Hemingway into a discussion of literature and authors. Finally, the eclectic conversation was postponed until the following day, and in parting, Kandisky remarked, "But it is a pleasure to meet one of the great old *Querschnitt* group."[17] That was one of the few times that Hemingway received recognition for his poetry, and it came on the plains of Kenya from a man who looked "like a caricature of [Robert] Benchley in Tyrolean costume. . . ." It was all "too fantastic to deal with."[18]

Besides the work that he sold to *Der Querschnitt* Hemingway also placed poetry in American little magazines during the 1920s. "Ultimately" appeared in the *Double-Dealer* (June 1922) with a poem by William Faulkner. Margaret Anderson accepted the ironic "They All Made Peace—What Is Peace?" for the *Little Review* (Spring 1923). And in the final issue of the magazine, she published Hemingway's broadside response to his first critics, "Valentine" (May 1929).

But during this period Hemingway wrote many more poems that he did not publish. A few are important to any consideration of what concerned the author during this time, and one of them affected his relationships with some Paris acquaintances and even, in a small way, his reputation.

When Hemingway read "To a Tragic Poetess"[19] at a party in October 1926, he angered some of his friends, including Donald Ogden Stewart and Archibald MacLeish, the host. They felt that the poem was a petulant and personal attack on Dorothy Parker. When Stewart rebuked Hemingway for the poem, Hemingway reacted by declaring their friendship to be over. The Paris to New York grapevine carried the news of the reading and the subsequent "breaking" of relationships, and the unpublished poem achieved notoriety by reputation alone. Hemingway has been criticized for his behavior in this matter, but he obviously felt strongly about what he had tried to express in "To a Tragic Poetess." Hemingway publicly ridiculed Parker's affairs, abortion, and suicide attempts.[20] Further, the poem is an attack on a writer who failed, in Hemingway's estimation, to see, to feel. It is an attack on sham self-destructiveness, especially when it is coupled with a lack of sympathy for others. Hemingway was particularly disgusted with Parker's histrionics. After offering such a sketch of this "tragic poetess," he recounted the tragedies of a few truly desperate men. Parker's self-described, and self-defeating, tragic qualities are diminished by comparison.

Hemingway addressed the issue of literature and its moral obligations in another long unpublished work, "Poem, 1928" (1929). Unlike "Valentine," this is a serious response to humanist academics and critics who were formulating some "new" theories that argued against writing based on experience. The experiences of the generation that had gone to war and had written about it were being dismissed by scholars. As Hemingway saw it, if the essence of his experience was going to last, it would be left to the children of these dogmatic critics to appreciate his work. In a less serious note to the next generation he passed on the tongue-in-cheek "Advice to a Son." This poem was published in Germany in 1932; it was the last poem that Hemingway published during his lifetime.

Hemingway apparently gave up writing poetry from 1935 until 1944; but when he turned to verse again, he developed a poetic form unlike anything he had ever done. During the late stages of World War II, Hemingway wrote long, personal, cathartic poems to Mary Welsh. In a similar mood, he wrote an assortment of poems in Paris during November and December 1949. For the most part, they were composed in his hotel room at the Ritz while he was finishing *Across the River and Into the Trees*. These poems are reminiscent of Colonel Richard Cantwell's mood in that ill-fated book. Despite their technical irregularities and obscurities, the poems that were written from 1944 to 1950 are painfully self-revealing; we are made to feel as though we are listening to a man talking to himself. For these poems, as for the story of Colonel Cantwell, a memory for experience and an insight into the nature of endurance are required. It is this sense of lonely endurance, every writer's lot, that is the subject of the last long poem he wrote. He borrowed a refrain from Kipling's poem "The Winners" to advise his friend Adriana Ivancich.[21] In "Lines to a Girl 5 Days After Her 21st Birthday" (1950) he gives his blessings to the young artist. But his advice to her lacks the playful irony of the earlier "Advice to a Son." He leaves her with the idea that what is most important is not to talk about work but to do it. And over everything comes the echo of Kipling's words: "She travels the fastest / Who travels alone."

Hemingway wrote most of his poems quickly in order to satisfy some immediate purpose. However, many of the manuscripts show signs of rewriting, and over half of the poems exist in more than one draft. The manuscripts that were produced during those odd creative moments have survived because Hemingway saved nearly every scrap of paper he ever used. These poems are as well-traveled as their creator; some have survived a war by lying peacefully forgotten in a trunk stored in the basement of the Paris Ritz; the paper clips have rusted on others as they waited in a back room at Sloppy Joe's Bar in Key West; some were rescued from Hemingway's home in Cuba; and a few were probably carried west to Ketchum, Idaho. Now, most of the surviving manuscripts are together at the John F. Kennedy Library in Boston, Massachusetts.

The poems have survived, but they are largely unknown. Much of the work in this collection appears for the first time. Furthermore, this is the first authorized American edition of Hemingway's previously published poems, many of which appeared originally in European magazines and expatriate small press editions half a century ago. Several of them were included in anthologies of the period, but these collections have long been out of print. Selections from Hemingway's poems have been translated into French, Italian, Russian, and Japanese. However, in this country, only odds and ends have been excerpted for critical and biographical studies with the only collected poems coming out in inaccurate, unauthorized editions.[22]

Despite limited critical attention, Hemingway's poetry has achieved a reputation for being obscene, a term that even he used to describe some of it. He took no pains to keep his language clean, and his satire was rough; respect did not come easily, and manners were not sacred. His satirical method tended to convert pretensions into sexual difficulties, as in "The Earnest Liberal's Lament" (1922). But the use of profanity and sexual allusions usually amounted to little more than barracks humor. The reactions in some of these poems reflect Hemingway's youthful sensibilities; he had felt bitterness as a boy, but after his experiences in World War I his disenchantment with conventional morality and its ineffectual language became firm. The world away from the front lines had been spared the horror of the war it had helped to create, but Hemingway saw no reason why refinement should exist hypocritically on one plane and foulness should be the condition of life on another. He brought a little piece of the war back to society.

In 1930, Louis Henry Cohn, Hemingway's first bibliographer, wanted to publish an American limited edition of a few poems. He was advised by John S. Sumner, Executive Secretary of the New York Society for the Suppression of Vice, that because certain words were used in the poems a copyright would not be issued.[23] Legally, Sumner had no control over copyrights; he could prevent the sale of a published work, but he could not prevent the issuance of a copyright. Cohn eventually printed a galley containing only four poems "for the prevention of piracy,"[24] but that action did not deter anyone from this practice.

Several pirated editions of Hemingway's published poems have appeared in the United States over the past thirty years,[25] and they have all played on the poems' ribald qualities. The pirates altered some of the titles and lines of the poems in order to achieve some weak humor, but the reason the poems were pirated in the first place was undoubtedly to exploit Hemingway's use of dirty words and to exploit his reputation. Hemingway's language does not shock contemporary literary tastes, but the presence of four-letter words in a pamphlet of poems written by a great writer, printed in a supposedly rare edition, and made more appealing by proclaiming itself to be pirated, all added up to an irresistible buy for thousands of readers. Under these less-than-serious conditions, how could Hemingway's poetry be considered honestly?

It would be a mistake to attribute much importance to these poems in the artistic development of Ernest Hemingway. Nevertheless, some critics have attempted to promote this argument. Hemingway could hardly have learned much about writing from working on the poems that he wrote in Chicago and Paris. He was a young writer—only twenty-two when he went to Paris—searching for a way to link language to his unique sensibilities. From what we know now about his literary style, it seems only natural that as a young man he would have attempted to work in poetic forms; the short lines, the concrete imagery, the potency of individual words, the rhythm, and the potential for achieving a condensed power in language must have appealed to him. But if his poetry was any kind of a beginning for him, it was a false beginning.

The true beginning—the writing of the work that would

last—came on a clear Paris morning in early 1922. Hemingway sat down at his work table, opened his notebook, and began to craft his "true sentences." He described how he came to write them in *A Moveable Feast*: "I would stand and look out over the roofs of Paris and think, 'Do not worry. You have always written before and you will write now. All you have to do is write one true sentence. Write the truest sentence that you know.' So finally I would write one true sentence, and then go on from there. It was easy then because there was always one true sentence that I knew or had seen or had heard someone say."[26] By April, he had worked out six of these lucid prose poems in his blue notebook.

Paris 1922, Auteiul Auteiul

I have seen the favourite crash into the Bulfinch and come down in a heap kicking; while the rest of the field swooped over the jump; the white wings jointing up their stretcher and the crowd raced across the pelouze to see the horses come into the stretch.

-//-

I have seen Peggy Joyce at 2 a.m. in a *Dancing* in the Rue Caumartin quarreling with the shellac haired young Chilean (who had manicured fingernails blew a puff of cigarette smoke into her face, wrote something in a note book) and shot himself at 3.30 the same morning.

-//-

I have watched the police charge the crowd with swords as they milled back into Paris through the Porte Maillot on the first of May and seen the frightened proud look on the white beaten-up face of the sixteen year old kid who looked like a prep school quarter back and had just shot two policemen.

-//-

I have stood on the crowded back platform of a seven
oclock Batignolles bus as it lurched along the wet
lamp lit street while men who were going home to
supper never looked up from their newspapers as we
passed Notre Dame grey and dripping in the rain.

-//-

I have seen the one legged street walker who works
the Boulevard Madelaine between the Rue Cambon
and Bernheim Jeune's limping along the pavement
through the crowd on a rainy night with a beefy
red-faced Episcopal clergyman holding an umbrella
over her.

-//-

I have watched two Senegalese soldiers in the dim
light of the snake house of the Jardin Des Plantes
teasing the King Cobra who swayed and tightened in
tense erect rage as one of the little brown men
crouched and feinted at him with his red fez.[27]

After the sentences came the paragraphs and the vignettes of
in our time; then the stories; then the novels. And because of
those writings—which are certainly poetic—the occasional
verse that Hemingway left behind has meaning and is
important.

In 1942 Wallace Stevens was asked to suggest someone to
lecture at Princeton on the poetic concept that he had called
"extraordinary actuality" (which he described as "conscious-
ness taking the place of imagination"). In his reply, Stevens
described the sort of person who could give the lecture and
named Hemingway as his first choice and added: "The
perception of the POETRY OF EXTRAORDINARY ACTUALITY is
. . . a job for a man capable of going his own way. . . . Most
people don't think of Hemingway as a poet, but obviously he is

a poet and I should say, offhand, the most significant of living poets, so far as the subject of EXTRAORDINARY ACTUALITY is concerned."[28] Of course, Stevens was writing about the poetic qualities of Hemingway's prose. But flashes of "extraordinary actuality" can be seen in Hemingway's poems.

Some of what is presented here is bawdy entertainment— and that is all it was meant to be. The poems do not represent Hemingway's mature style. But, as is often the case with posthumous publications of lesser works, the reader recognizes the man beyond the myth. Ezra Pound once said of his friend Ernest Hemingway, "The son of a bitch's *instincts* are right!"[29] Much of what was good about those instincts can be seen in these poems. They are direct, often quick, ribald, but sometimes moving reflections of the man. They lack the subtlety, psychological complexity, and beauty of the prose. But there is no mistaking their messages.

The Text

The poems are arranged in the probable order of composition. In some cases evidence provided by handwriting, paper, typewriter faces, and content has been used to assign a date of composition. The probable place and date of composition, followed by first and important publications, are provided at the end of each poem, thus:

> Oak Park, 1917
> *Tabula* (March 1917)

The notes section provides background and explanatory information.

When a poem was not titled by Hemingway, its first line has been used in brackets as the title. In cases where the text of the poem has been transcribed from a manuscript, the editor has of necessity made judgments concerning the readings. Hemingway's handwriting is difficult; for example, he did not clearly or consistently differentiate capital and lowercase letters, and the placement of his punctuation marks is sometimes puzzling. Since some of the manuscripts—particularly for the late poems—were written under difficult circumstances, the form or structure of a poem is not always clear. Specimen manuscript pages are provided to acquaint the reader with some of the transcription difficulties presented by Hemingway's hand.

The poems published here are emended reading texts. In each case the poem has been edited from the surviving form (manuscript, typescript, or print) closest to the author's final intention. See Nicholas Gerogiannis, "Editorial Apparatus for *88 Poems*," *Fitzgerald/Hemingway Annual 1979,* for a record of the editorial emendations; this article lists all the surviving manuscripts and typescripts for each poem, as well as publications in English. For each poem the "Apparatus" stipulates the copy-text (the version that has been selected by the editor as the basis for the corrected text published in this volume).

Notes

[1]Known now simply as *Poetry.* This was—and is—considered a major publication for a young poet.

[2]This is the bulk of EH's existing poetic works. Because of their private nature, four poems were not made available for publication by Mary Welsh Hemingway, executrix of the estate. They are "Lines to a Great Beauty," "Lines to his very beautiful wife," "Lines to M. and her surgeon," and "Grosshau"—items #157-160 in Philip Young and Charles W. Mann's *The Hemingway Manuscripts: An Inventory* (University Park: Pennsylvania State University Press, 1969), p. 78. The editor was charged by Mrs. Hemingway to omit anything that might injure a living person, and a fifth poem was withheld as a result; this is "Hurray for Fonnie Richardson" (Young & Mann, #184, p. 83). Mrs. Hemingway's permission to publish her husband's poems has been as liberal as possible. There is one other omission: "Storm Troops" (Young & Mann, #181, p. 82) could not be located in EH's private papers

nor at the Hemingway Collection in the John F. Kennedy Library.

One cannot be certain that there are not more undiscovered poems. EH sometimes included verse in his correspondence. And there are other stranger possibilities. In 1977 a CBS news team was touring Cuba. During one broadcast the newscaster pointed out a poem scribbled on the wall of a Havana bar. The popular belief is, he said, that EH wrote it. Another interesting cache of material is a small group of poems that EH gave to his friend Marlene Dietrich in the late 1940s. Their titles have not been verified, but the editor suspects that these are the poems EH wrote at the Ritz Hotel in 1944 and 1949 and which are in the fourth section of this book.

[3]EH's lost novel.

[4]Gertrude Stein, *The Autobiography of Alice B. Toklas* (New York: Harcourt, Brace, 1933), pp. 260-261.

[5]"Hugh Selwyn Mauberly."

[6]EH to Lewis Galantière, Carlos Baker, *Ernest Hemingway: A Life Story* (New York: Scribners, 1969), p. 86.

[7]Baker, p. 123.

[8]There are several accounts of this. EH wrote about it in *A Moveable Feast* (New York: Scribners, 1964), p. 74.

[9]Charles A. Fenton, *The Apprenticeship of Ernest Hemingway* (New York: Farrar, Straus & Young, 1954), p. 226.

[10]Fenton, p. 225. Fenton comments: "Hemingway himself has dated his work as beginning with *Three Stories & Ten Poems.*"

[11]Edmund Wilson, *The Shores of Light* (New York: Farrar, Straus & Young, 1952), p. 117.

[12]Edmund Wilson, "Mr. Hemingway's Dry-Points," *Dial*, 77 (October 1924): 340-341.

[13]Baker, p. 118.

[14]George Antheil, *Bad Boy of Music* (New York: Doubleday, Doran, 1945), p. 147.

[15]Eugene Jolas, "Open Letter to Ernest Hemingway," *Chicago Tribune*, European Edition, Sunday Magazine, 16 November 1924, p. 2.

[16]*Green Hills of Africa* (New York: Scribners, 1935), p. 7.

[17]*Green Hills of Africa*, p. 8.

[18]*Green Hills of Africa*, pp. 9-10.

[19]For a fuller explanation of this affair, with references, see the notes to "To a Tragic Poetess" (poem 67).

[20]John Keats, *You Might As Well Live: The Life and Times of Dorothy Parker* (New York: Simon & Schuster, 1970), pp. 90-92.

[21]She is widely accepted as the model for Renata in *Across the River and Into the Trees*. EH's poem to Adriana helps to clarify his relationship with the young woman.

[22]The unauthorized editions, selling for from 50¢ to $35, contain eighteen poems—most of EH's poetry published while he was living in Paris in the 1920s. Unfortunately, most of the critical work on the published poems has been based on the unauthorized versions, which are pockmarked by errors. The pirates have also done a steady business with professors who order their books for college courses; but critics and professors cannot be blamed because copies of the original publications are rare.

[23]Audre Hanneman, *Ernest Hemingway: A Comprehensive Bibliography* (Princeton: Princeton University Press, 1967), p. 266.

[24]Ernest Hemingway, *Four Poems* (12 copies privately printed by Louis Henry Cohn, 31 August 1930).

[25]There are seven unauthorized editions (lettered A-G) listed in Hanneman, pp. 68-70, and in Hanneman's *Supplement* (Princeton: Princeton University Press, 1975), pp. 12-14. The following are the editions of EH's poetry that appeared in *Books In Print 1977-1978*. Two of these entries do not appear in Hanneman's bibliography, which brings the total number of known unauthorized editions to nine.

    Collected Poems (San Francisco: City Lights, 1960). 50¢, Hanneman C.
    Collected Poems (New York: Haskell House, 1970). $8.95, Hanneman E.
    The Collected Poems of Ernest Hemingway (New York: Gordon Press, 1972). $34.95.
    The Collected Poems of Ernest Hemingway (Folcroft, Pa.: Folcroft Library Editions, n.d.). $8.50.

[26]*A Moveable Feast*, p. 12.

[27]First published with minor omissions in Baker, pp. 90-91.

[28]Wallace Stevens, *The Letters of Wallace Stevens*, ed. Holly Stevens (New York: Knopf, 1966), pp. 411-412.

[29]Archibald MacLeish, "His Mirror Was Danger," *Life*, 51 (14 July 1961): 71.

Ernest Hemingway
Complete Poems

Juvenilia

1912-1917

Apr. 12. '12   Ernestt
                    The opening game.

I ST   Inning.

With Chance on first, and Evers on Third,
    Great things from the Cubs will be heard.
Then up comes Saulte to the bat.
    On the plate his bat does rap;
Takes a slug at that old ball,
    Makes it clear the right field
wall.
            Then in Comes Chance and
In comes Evers,
    Such hits are seldom seen—
most never.
            Then to the bat comes Tim
In haste,
    He sure knows how the ball
to past.
He slams that ball upon the
Bean,
    And seems to make it scream
The Center fielder nabs the ball;
It seems as if 'twould make him
fall.
            over on top of next page.

Hemingway's first surviving poem, 1912.

1   The Opening Game

1st Inning

With Chance on first, and Evers on third,
   Great things from the Cubs will soon be heard.
Then up comes Schulte to the bat,
   On the plate his bat does rap;
Takes a slug at that old ball,
   Makes it clear the right field wall.
Then in comes Chance and in comes Evers,
   Such hits are seldom seen—'most never.
Then to the bat comes Zim in haste,
   He sure knows how the ball to paste.
He slams that ball upon the Bean,
   Almost seems to make it scream.
The center fielder nabs the ball;
   It seems as if 't'would make him fail.
But stop of this rank stuff,
   Just one inning is enough.

Oak Park, 12 April 1912

A4e
13

2 [Blank Verse]

"   "
          !   :   ,   .
                  ,   ,   ,   .
        ,   ;   !
                      ,

Oak Park, 1916
Trapeze (10 November 1916)

3   Dedicated to F. W.

Lives of football men remind us,
  We can dive and kick and slug,
And departing leave behind us,
  Hoof prints on another's mug.

Oak Park, 1916
Trapeze (24 November 1916)

FRED WILCOXEN
HIGH SCHOOL
BUDDY AND
FELLOW
NEWSPAPER
STAFFER

4 How Ballad Writing Affects Our Seniors

Oh, I've never writ a ballad
And I'd rather eat shrimp salad,
(Tho' the Lord knows how I hate the
   Pink and scrunchy little beasts),
But Miss Dixon says I gotto—
(And I pretty near forgotto)
But I'm sitting at my table
   And my feet are pointing east.

Now one stanza, it is over—
Oh! Heck, what rhymes with "over"?
Ah! yes; "I'm now in clover,"
But when I've got that over
I don't yet know what to write.
I might write of young Lloyd Boyle,
Sturdy son of Irish soil,
But to write of youthful Boyle
Would involve increasing toil,
For there is so much material
I'd never get it done.

Somewhere in this blessed metre
There's a crook. The stanzas peter
Out before I get them started
   Just like that one did, just then.
But I'll keep a-writing on
Just in hope some thought will strike me.
When it does, I'll let it run
   Just in splashes off my pen.

(Wish that blamed idea would come.)
I've been writing for two pages,
But it seems like countless ages,
    For I've scribbled and I've scribbled,
But I haven't said a thing.
This is getting worse each minute,
For whatever I put in it
    I shall have to read before the English class.

'Know where I would like to be—
Just a-lyin' 'neath a tree
Watchin' clouds up in the sky—
Fleecy clouds a-sailin' by
And we'd look up in the blue—
Only me, an' maybe you.
I could write a ballad then
That would drip right off my pen.
    (Aw, shucks!)

For the future I shall promise
    (If you let me live this time),
I'll ne'er write another ballad—
    Never venture into rhyme.

Oak Park, 1916
Tabula (November 1916)

5 The Worker

Far down in the sweltering guts of the ship
  The stoker swings his scoop
Where the jerking hands of the steam gauge drive
And muscles and tendons and sinews rive;
While it's hotter than hell to a man alive,
  He toils in his sweltering coop.

He is baking and sweating his life away
  In that blasting roar of heat;
But he's fighting a battle with wind and tide,
All to the end that you may ride;
And through it all he is living beside;
  He can work and sleep and eat.

Oak Park, 1917
Tabula (March 1917)

Athletic Verse
Ernest Hemingway, '17, and Fred Wilcoxen, '17

6   The Tackle

Two big red fists pawing the air,
  A drawn, sweat-stained face,
Tufts of blonde hair sticking out of a yellow headguard,
  Long gorilla arms, reaching and reaching,
A heaving, gasping chest,
  Alert, shifting mud-stained legs.
A quick pull, a thrust, a headlong dive at a
Group of rushing legs.
  A crashing, rocking jar,
And the crowd yells:
  "Yeah! Threw him for a two yard loss!"

7   The Punt

Twenty-two mud-daubed figures battling together on a
    muddy field.
  A sharp barking of numbers,
The front line of figures pile up together,
The back line crouch and throw themselves
  At the men coming through.
The sodden thump of a pigskin being kicked,
  And the ball rises higher and higher in the air
While the grimy, muddy figures race down the field.

8 The Safety Man

Standing, a little figure alone in the middle of a
    white-lined field,
Two stands full of faces rise to their feet with
  A mighty roar.
A grey figure whirls free of the tumbled line of scrimmage.
  He tears straight down the field,
His flying feet thudding over the white lines.
The safety man poises, then shoots forward;
  He brings the grey sweatered man to the ground with a crash.
Cole is on the job.

Oak Park, 1917
Tabula (March 1917)

9 The Inexpressible

When the June bugs were a-circlin'
   Round the arc light on the corner
And a-makin' shooty shadows on the street;
   When you strolled along barefooted
Through a warm dark night of June
   Where the dew from off the cool grass bathed your feet—

When you heard a banjo thunkin'
   On the porch across the road,
And you smelled the scent of lilacs in the park
   There was something struggling in you
That you couldn't put in words—
   You was really livin' poetry in the dark!

Oak Park, 1917
Tabula (March

Wanderings

1918-1925

VOLUME NO I   MAY 27   ISSUE NO 2

SPECIAL POETRY NUMBER OF LA PACKAGE .

P^etic supplement .

THE SHIP   TRANSLATED BEING LA PAQUEBOT .

THE SHIP DOETH PITCH
LIKE A SON OF A BITCH

editors note   this poem was awarded the
Grand Prix .

French edition

La Bateau
roquet likee
fellet de canine .
THE TALE OF ARGYLE

In the morning did the passengers
Seek to bolt the massive foodstuffs
Came the duke
Ee of Argyle
Downed the cornbeef
Downed the salad
Came unto the great roast porker
Got it in his mouth and half way
Down his gullet got it got it ,
Then it rose
He wo uld of straggled
But he rushed forth from the salon
Moved by motives philanthropic
Sought to furnish food for fishes ,
Here we draw the curtain readers
Here we draw the baleful cirtain .
We will tell not of his pukings
Of his retchings and his gobbings
Nay we will not gentle reader .
WE WILL TELL NOT OF THE BUNTIN
Shooting forth t e pale green mixture
Like the clam juice flecked with syrup .
Or of Fritz the noted Smagel
Bringing forth the whole oranges .
Or of captain Pease the easily heard
What he puketh forth we tell not
For wefear it hurteth discipline .
So we leave you gentle reader
We must seek a can
Or washbowl .

Typescript, "The Ship   Translated Being La Paquebot," 1918.
Collection of W. Jones.

10 The Ship Translated Being La Paquebot

In the morning did the passengers
   Seek to bolt the massive foodstuffs
Came the duke
   He of Argyle
Downed the cornbeef
    Downed the salad
   Came unto the great roast porker
    Got it in his mouth and half way
   Down his gullet got it got it,
Then it rose
    He would of strangled
   But he rushed forth from the salon
  Moved by motives philanthropic
    Sought to furnish food for fishes,
   Here we draw the curtain readers
Here we draw the baleful curtain.
    We will tell not of his pukings
   Of his retchings and his gobbings
    Nay we will not gentle reader.
    WE WILL TELL NOT OF THE BUNTIN
  Shooting forth the pale green mixture
    Like the clam juice flecked with syrup.
Or of Fritz the noted Spiegel
    Bringing forth the whole oranges.
  Or of Captain Pease the easily heard
     What he puketh forth we tell not
   For we fear it hurteth discipline.
  So we leave you gentle reader
    We must seek a can
   Or washbowl.

Aboard the *Chicago*, 1918
Fitzgerald/Hemingway Annual 1972

11 [There was Ike and Tony and Jaque and me ...]

There was Ike and Tony and Jaque and me
   Roarin thru Schio town
Three days leave and a'feelin free
Well puffed up but we still could see
  We were lookin 'em up and down.
    Especially up and down.

For a face don't matter on three days' leave
To Ike or Tony or Jaque or me.
You can look at a face, an a face is free
  But an ankle's somethin' to make you grieve
    For an ankle's an indication.

Cognac's good if it ain't Martel,
And an ankle has secrets it doesn't tell.
  Sometimes it keeps them, but buy and sell.
Three days more we'll be back in hell
  So we don't give a damn if she ain't Martel.

. . . .

ca. 1918-1920

18

12 A Modern Version of Polonius' Advice

Give thy tongue no tho'ts,
Nor ever think before you speak,
Lest folks suspecium that thou art a highbrow.
Those friends thou has that keep their purse strings tied,
Beware and shun them most decidedly.

. . . .

ca. 1920

13 [In a magazine ...]

In a magazine
I saw a picture of a trench club,
Studded with iron knobs
And a steel spike on the end.
I thought:
My Gawd, but that would balance great;
And I itched to swing it
And feel it crunch on the head of some Hun—
Preferably unarmed—
And another,
And another, and another.
Gawd, wouldn't it be great?
—To smash the skull,
And the blood spurt out like killing beeves at the
    Stock Yards?
If they cried "Kamerad,"
Swing!
The same afternoon I saw
A tall blond, a fresh faced Swede,
Drunk, he resisted three policemen
Trying to drag him out of a motor.
A big "bull" swung his club against the boy's head,
The crack sounded like a two bagger;
Not the sullen "whunk" of a blackjack,
But a crack.
Then they all clubbed him and he fell,
They dragged him up a stairway,
His bloody face bumping, bumping, bumping,
On the stairs.
Jesus Christ! Is this the I who wanted
To use
A trench club?

ca. 1920

14   **To Will Davies**

There were two men to be hanged
To be hanged by the neck until dead
A judge had said so
A judge with a black cap.
One of them had to be held up
Standing on the drop in the high corridor of the county jail.
He drooled from his mouth and slobber ran down his chin
And he fell all over the priest who was talking fast into
    his ear
In a language he didn't understand.
I was glad when they pulled the black bag over his face.
The other was a nigger
Standing straight and dignified like the doorman at the
    Blackstone
"No Sah—Ah aint got nuthin to say."
It gave me a bad moment,
I felt sick at my stomach
I was afraid they were hanging Bert Williams.

ca. 1920

15   The Battle of Copenhagen

It's always been a mystery
Why there's no word in history
　　　of the Battle of Copenhagen.

There's never been a parallel
So far as ever I've heard tell
To the fighting and the biting
And the smashing and the crashing
And the lashing and the slashing
And the gnashing and the gashing,
To the yellishness and smellishness
And international hellishness
　　　of the Battle of Copenhagen.

　　　*　*　*

Ten thousand stalwart Swedes
Advancing through the weeds
　　　to the Battle of Copenhagen.

Unlimited Italians
In column of batallions
　　　at the Battle of Copenhagen.

Ten tribes of red Pawnees
Were sulking behind trees
　　　at the Battle of Copenhagen.

A platoon of Albanians,
Supported by Ukranians
And also some Roumanians,
The dull ones and the brainy ones,
　　　at the Battle of Copenhagen.

Three thousand greasy Greeks,
Arrayed in leathern breeks
And smelling strong of leeks,
            at the Battle of Copenhagen.

A quantity of Turks
All waving bloody dirks
            at the Battle of Copenhagen.

Six hundred Abyssinians,
The fat ones and the skinny ones;
Two hundred of the Czeck
With their battle cry, "By Hzeck!"
            at the Battle of Copenhagen.

Eighteen hundred Scots,
Their plaidies tied in knots
And dangling pewter pots
(The dirty, low-down sots!)
            at the Battle of Copenhagen.

Two hundred Asiatics
In vari-colored Batiks—
A company of Japs
Bravely shooting craps—
A myriad of Mongolians,
The sinful and the holy ones,
With their friends, two Anatolians
            at the Battle of Copenhagen.

                *   *   *

From out the Boreal Regions
Came a handful of Norwegians
To oppose these countless legions
            in the Battle of Copenhagen.

* * *

A half a million Jews
Ran back to tell the news
            of the Battle of Copenhagen.

Chicago, 1920-1921

16 Oklahoma

All of the Indians are dead
(A good Indian is a dead Indian)
Or riding in motor cars.
(The oil lands, you know, they're all rich)
Smoke smarts my eyes,
Cottonwood twigs and buffalo dung
Smoke grey in the teepee—
(Or is it myopic trachoma?)

The prairies are long,
The moon rises,
Ponies
Drag at their pickets.
The grass has gone brown in the summer—
(Or is it the hay crop failing?)

Pull an arrow out,
If you break it
The wound closes.
Salt is good too
And wood ashes.
Pounding it throbs in the night—
(Or is it the gonorrhea)

Chicago, 1920-1921
Three Stories & Ten Poems (1923)

17 Captives

Some came in chains
Unrepentant but tired.
Too tired but to stumble.
Thinking and hating were finished
Thinking and fighting were finished
Retreating and hoping were finished.
Cures thus a long campaign,
Making death easy.

Chicago, 1920–1921
Three Stories & Ten Poems (1923)

18 Champs d'Honneur

Soldiers never do die well;
  Crosses mark the places,
Wooden crosses where they fell;
  Stuck above their faces.
Soldiers pitch and cough and twitch;
  All the world roars red and black,
Soldiers smother in a ditch;
  Choking through the whole attack.

Chicago, 1920-1921
Poetry (January 1923)
Three Stories & Ten Poems (1923)

27

19   D'Annunzio

Half a million dead wops
And he got a kick out of it
The son of a bitch.

Chicago, 1920-1921

20 [God is away for the summer ...]

SOCIETY COLUMN—The Reverend John Timothy Stone, pastor of the
Fourth Presbyterian Church, has gone to the Colorado Mountains
for the summer.

God is away for the summer
The city swelters along without him.
Children cry in the hot nights
Keeping men awake who must go to work in the morning.
The burlesque houses are closed by the heat
Plump women don't look good
In hot weather
Even to the men who frequent the Star and Garter.
John Timothy Stone has followed Him up into the mountains.
In the fall he will be back
He will bring the word of God from the mountains
God never leaves the city for long.

Chicago, 1920-1921

21   Flat Roofs

It is cool at night on the roofs of the city
The city sweats
Dripping and stark.
Maggots of life
Crawl in the hot loneliness of the city.
Love curdles in the city
Love sours in the hot whispering from the pavements.
Love grows old
Old with the oldness of sidewalks.
It is cool at night on the roofs of the city.

Chicago, 1921

22 [Night comes with soft and drowsy plumes . . .]

Night comes with soft and drowsy plumes
To darken out the day
To stroke away the flinty glint
Softening out the clay
Before the final hardness comes
Demanding that we stay.

Chicago, 1920-1921

23 [At night I lay with you . . .]

At night I lay with you
And watched
The city whirl and spin about

Chicago, 1920-1921

24 Lines to a Young Lady on Her Having Very Nearly Won a Vögel

Through the hot, pounding rhythm of the waltz
You swung and whirled with eager, pagan grace
Two sleepy birds
Preen in their wicker cages
And I
Am dancing with a woman of the town.

Chicago, 1921

25 Chapter Heading

For we have thought the longer thoughts
  And gone the shorter way.
And we have danced to devils' tunes,
  Shivering home to pray;
To serve one master in the night,
  Another in the day.

Chicago, 1921
Poetry (January 1923)
Three Stories & Ten Poems (1923)

26 Killed   Piave—July 8—1918

Desire and
All the sweet pulsing aches
And gentle hurtings
That were you,
Are gone into the sullen dark.
Now in the night you come unsmiling
To lie with me
A dull, cold, rigid bayonet
On my hot-swollen, throbbing soul.

Chicago, 1921

27 Bird of Night

Cover my eyes with your pinions
Dark bird of night
Spread your black wings like a turkey strutting
Drag your strong wings like a cock grouse drumming
Scratch the smooth flesh of my belly
With scaly claws
Dip with your beak to my lips
But cover my eyes with your pinions.

Chicago, 1921

28 Mitrailliatrice

The mills of the gods grind slowly;
But this mill
Chatters in mechanical staccato.
Ugly short infantry of the mind,
Advancing over difficult terrain,
Make this Corona
Their mitrailleuse.

Chicago, 1921
Poetry (January 1923)
Three Stories & Ten Poems (1923)

29   [On Weddynge Gyftes]

Three traveling clocks
Tick
On the mantelpiece
Comma
But the young man is starving.

Chicago, 1921
Toronto Star Weekly
(17 December 1921)

The Toronto Star Weekly, Saturday, December 17, 1921.

30 Ultimately

He tried to spit out the truth;
Dry mouthed at first,
He drooled and slobbered in the end;
Truth dribbling his chin.

ca. 1921
Double-Dealer (June 1922)

31 [FOR THE HARLOT HAS A HARDLOT . . .]

FOR THE HARLOT HAS A HARDLOT
SYPHYLLIS IS HER END
AND THE HARLOTS PORK
DOES A LOT OF DIRTY WORK
AND THE HARLOTS DOG AINT WELL.

Paris, 1922

32   ["Blood is thicker than water . . ."]

"Blood is thicker than water,"
The young man said
As he knifed his friend
For a drooling old bitch
And a house full of lies.

Paris, 1922
Ernest Hemingway: A Life Story (1969)

33 [All armies are the same . . .]

All armies are the same
Publicity is fame
Artillery makes the same old noise
Valor is an attribute of boys
Old soldiers all have tired eyes
All soldiers hear the same old lies
Dead bodies always have drawn flies

Paris, ca. 1922

34 Shock Troops

Men went happily to death
But they were not the men
Who marched
For years
Up to the line.
These rode a few times
And were gone
Leaving a heritage of obscene song.

Paris, ca. 1922

35 Oily Weather

The sea desires deep hulls—
It swells and rolls.
The screw churns a throb—
Driving, throbbing, progressing.
The sea rolls with love,
Surging, caressing,
Undulating its great loving belly.
The sea is big and old—
Throbbing ships scorn it.

Paris, ca. 1922
Poetry (January 1923)
Three Stories & Ten Poems (1923)

36 Roosevelt

Workingmen believed
He busted trusts,
And put his picture in their windows.
"What he'd have done in France!"
They said.
Perhaps he would—
He could have died
Perhaps,
Though generals rarely die except in bed,
As he did finally.
And all the legends that he started in his life
Live on and prosper,
Unhampered now by his existence.

Paris, 1922
Poetry (January 1923)
Three Stories & Ten Poems (1923)

37 Riparto d'Assalto

Drummed their boots on the camion floor,
Hob-nailed boots on the camion floor.
Sergeants stiff,
Corporals sore.
Lieutenants thought of a Mestre whore—
Warm and soft and sleepy whore,
Cozy, warm and lovely whore:
Damned cold, bitter, rotten ride,
Winding road up the Grappa side.
Arditi on benches stiff and cold,
Pride of their country stiff and cold,
Bristly faces, dirty hides—
Infantry marches, Arditi rides.
Grey, cold, bitter, sullen ride—
To splintered pines on the Grappa side
At Asalone, where the truck-load died.

Paris, 1922
Poetry (January 1923)
Three Stories & Ten Poems (1923)

38 To Good Guys Dead

They sucked us in;
King and country,
Christ Almighty
And the rest.
Patriotism,
Democracy,
Honor—
Words and phrases,
They either bitched or killed us.

Paris, ca. 1922

My love walked there.

And every hut in Lombardy
was
~~was~~ Like a bit of Arcady
My love ~~walked~~ was there.

Arsiero, Asiago,
Twice
~~of~~ a hundred more,
Nameless little villages,
Back before the war a

~~How ...~~
~~Lot of ...~~
White washed plaster houses,
~~Narrow~~ Vastly cobbled streets
Women in the door ways
Bare armed peeling beets;
Santa Caterina Poena (and Such)
~~And~~ Not in the geographies
~~Back~~ Long before the war.
~~...~~ ~~...~~ ~~...~~

Working draft, "[Arsiero, Asiago . . .]" ca. 1922.

39 [Arsiero, Asiago . . .]

Arsiero, Asiago,
   Half a hundred more,
Little border villages,
   Back before the war,
Monte Grappa, Monte Corno,
   Twice a dozen such,
In the piping times of peace
   Didn't come to much.

Paris, ca. 1922

40 Montparnasse

There are never any suicides in the quarter among people
  one knows
No successful suicides.
A Chinese boy kills himself and is dead.
(they continue to place his mail in the letter rack
  at the Dome)
A Norwegian boy kills himself and is dead.
(no one knows where the other Norwegian boy has gone)
They find a model dead
alone in bed and very dead.
(it made almost unbearable trouble for the concierge)
Sweet oil, the white of eggs, mustard and water, soap suds
and stomach pumps rescue the people one knows.
Every afternoon the people one knows can be found at
  the cafe.

Paris, 1922
Three Stories & Ten Poems (1923)

41 Along With Youth

A porcupine skin,
Stiff with bad tanning,
It must have ended somewhere.
Stuffed horned owl
Pompous
Yellow eyed;
Chuck-wills-widow on a biased twig
Sooted with dust.
Piles of old magazines,
Drawers of boys' letters
And the line of love
They must have ended somewhere.
Yesterday's *Tribune* is gone
Along with youth
And the canoe that went to pieces on the beach
The year of the big storm
When the hotel burned down
At Seney, Michigan.

Paris, 1922
Three Stories & Ten Poems (1923)

42 The Earnest Liberal's Lament

I know monks masturbate at night,
That pet cats screw,
That some girls bite,
And yet
What can I do
To set things right?

Paris, 1922
Querschnitt (Autumn 1924)

43 The Age Demanded

The age demanded that we sing
and cut away our tongue.
The age demanded that we flow
and hammered in the bung.
The age demanded that we dance
and jammed us into iron pants.
And in the end the age was handed
the sort of shit that it demanded.

Paris, 1922
Querschnitt (February 1925)

44 Kipling

There's a little monkey maiden looking eastward toward
the sea,
   There's a new monkey soprano a'sobbing in the tree,
And Harold's looking very fit the papers all agree.

L'Envoi

It was quite an operation,
   But it may have saved the nation,
And what's one amputation
   To the tribe?

Paris, ca. 1922

45 Stevenson

Under the wide and starry sky,
  Give me new glands and let me lie,
Oh how I try and try and try,
  But I need much more than a will.

Paris, ca. 1922

46 Robert Graves

Glands for the financier,
Flags for the Fusilier,
For English poets beer,
Strong beer for me.

Paris, ca. 1922

47 [I'm off'n wild wimmen . . .]

I'm off'n wild wimmen
An Cognac
An Sinnin'
For I'm in loOOOOOOOve.

Paris, ca. 1922

48 [Grass smooth on the prairies . . .]

Grass smooth on the prairies
  Plows breaking
Streets smooth and shining
  Trucks crumbling.
Asphalt, tell me what follows the asphalt.
Wops, he said, wops follow the asphalt.

Paris, ca. 1922

49   Translations from the Esquimaux

There Are Seasons

The sea otter dived;
The sea is oil under the moon.
The sea otter dived;
It was cold and the swells were long.

Paris, ca. 1922

Working draft, "Poem," ca. 1922.

50 Poem

The only man I ever loved
Said good bye
And went away
He was killed in Picardy
On a sunny day.

Paris, ca. 1922

51 Schwarzwald

As white hairs in a silver fox's skin
The birches lie against the dark pine hill
They're talking German in the compartment
Now we're winding up
Through tunnels
Puffing
Dark valleys, noisy rivered
Rock filled, barred with white.
Heavy browed houses
Green fields,
Forested with hop poles
A flock of geese along the road.
I knew a gypsy once who said
He hoped to die here.

Paris or Germany, 1922

52 They All Made Peace—What Is Peace?

All of the turks are gentlemen and Ismet Pasha is a little
deaf. But the Armenians. How about the Armenians?
Well the Armenians.

Lord Curzon likes young boys.
So does Chicherin.
So does Mustapha Kemal. He is good looking too. His eyes
are too close together but he makes war. That is the way
he is.

Lord Curzon does not love Chicherin. Not at all. His beard
trickles and his hands are cold. He thinks all the time.

Lord Curzon thinks too. But he is much taller and goes to
St. Moritz.

Mr. Child does not wear a hat.
Baron Hayashi gets in and out of the automobile.
Monsieur Barrèré gets telegrams. So does Marquis Garroni.
His telegrams come on motorcycles from MUSSOLINI.
MUSSOLINI has nigger eyes and a bodyguard and has his
picture taken reading a book upside down. MUSSOLINI is
wonderful. Read the Daily Mail.

I used to know Mussolini. Nobody liked him then. Even I
didn't like him. He was a bad character. Ask Monsieur
Barrèré.

We all drink cocktails. Is it too early to have a cocktail?
How about a drink George? Come on and we'll have a cocktail
Admiral. Just time before lunch. Well what if we do? Not
too dry.

Well what do you boys know this morning?

Oh they're shrewd. They're shrewd.

Who have we got in on the subcommission this morning,
Admiral?

M. Stambuliski walks up the hill and down the hill. Don't talk
about M. Venizelos. He is wicked. You can see it. His beard
shows it.
Mr. Child is not wicked.
Mrs. Child has flat breasts and Mr. Child is an idealist and
wrote Harding's campaign speeches and calls Senator
Beveridge Al.
You know me Al.
Lincoln Steffens is with Child. The big C. makes the joke easy.

Then there is Mosul
And the Greek Patriarch
What about the Greek Patriarch?

Paris-Lausanne, 1922
Little Review (Spring 1923)

53 I Like Americans

By A Foreigner

I like Americans.
They are so unlike Canadians.
They do not take their policemen seriously.
They come to Montreal to drink.
Not to criticize.
They claim they won the war.
But they know at heart that they didn't.
They have such respect for Englishmen.
They like to live abroad.
They do not brag about how they take baths.
But they take them.
Their teeth are so good.
And they wear B.V.D.'s all the year round.
I wish they didn't brag about it.
They have the second best navy in the world.
But they never mention it.
They would like to have Henry Ford for president.
But they will not elect him.
They saw through Bill Bryan.
They have gotten tired of Billy Sunday.
Their men have such funny hair cuts.
They are hard to suck in on Europe.
They have been there once.
They produced Barney Google, Mutt and Jeff.
And Jiggs.
They do not hang lady murderers.
They put them in vaudeville.
They read the Saturday Evening Post
And believe in Santa Claus.
When they make money
They make a lot of money.
They are fine people.

ca. 1923
Toronto Star Weekly (unlocated clipping)

54 I Like Canadians

By A Foreigner

I like Canadians.
They are so unlike Americans.
They go home at night.
Their cigarets don't smell bad.
Their hats fit.
They really believe that they won the war.
They don't believe in Literature.
They think Art has been exaggerated.
But they are wonderful on ice skates.
A few of them are very rich.
But when they are rich they buy more horses
Than motor cars.
Chicago calls Toronto a puritan town.
But both boxing and horse-racing are illegal
In Chicago.
Nobody works on Sunday.
Nobody.
That doesn't make me mad.
There is only one Woodbine.
But were you ever at Blue Bonnets?
If you kill somebody with a motor car in Ontario
You are liable to go to jail.
So it isn't done.
There have been over 500 people killed by motor cars
In Chicago
So far this year.
It is hard to get rich in Canada.
But it is easy to make money.
There are too many tea rooms.
But, then, there are no cabarets.
If you tip a waiter a quarter
He says "Thank you."
Instead of calling the bouncer.

They let women stand up in the street cars.
Even if they are good-looking.
They are all in a hurry to get home to supper
And their radio sets.
They are a fine people.
I like them.

ca. 1923
Toronto Star Weekly (unlocated clipping)

55 The Big Dance on the Hill

The arrival.
The vast crowd on the floor.
The encounter with the boss.
The man to man smile from the boss.
The feeling of elation.
The door keeper from the office who is serving out.
The whisper from the door keeper.
The long journey down the hall.
The closed door.
The clink of glasses.
The opening of the door.
The imposing array of glassware.
The sight of the host.
The look on the host's face.
The sight of the boss with the host.
The look on the boss' face.
The sight of several other distinguished looking men.
The look on the distinguished looking men's faces.
The atmosphere of disapproval.
The request from the attendant.
The giving of the order.
The silent consumption of the order.
The silence kept by the host, the boss and the distinguished
   looking men.
The uncomfortable feeling.
The increase of the uncomfortable feeling.
The retreat.
The journey down the long hallway.
The chuckles from the door keeper.
The statement by the door keeper that he had been instructed
   to admit only the family and old friends.
The renewed chuckles by the door keeper.
The desire to kill the door keeper.
The sad return to the dance floor.

ca. 1923
Toronto Star Weekly (24 November 1923)

56 The Sport of Kings

The friend who calls up over the telephone.
The horse that has been especially wired from Pimlico.
The letting in of the friends in the office.
The search for ready money.
The studying of the entries.
The mysterious absence from the office.
The time of suspense and waiting.
The feeling of excitement among the friends in the office.
The trip outside to buy a sporting extra.
The search for the results.
The sad return upstairs.
The hope that the paper may have made a mistake.
The feeling among the friends in the office that the paper
   is right.
The attitude of the friends in the office.
The feeling of remorse.
The lightened pay envelope.

ca. 1923
Toronto Star Weekly (24 November 1923)

57 The Soul of Spain with McAlmon and Bird the Publishers

In the rain in the rain in the rain in the rain in Spain.
Does it rain in Spain?
Oh yes my dear on the contrary and there are no bull fights.
The dancers dance in long white pants
It isn't right to yence your aunts
Come Uncle, let's go home.
Home is where the heart is, home is where the fart is.
Come let us fart in the home.
There is no art in a fart.
Still a fart may not be artless.
Let us fart and artless fart in the home.
Democracy.
Democracy.
Bill says democracy must go.
Go democracy
Go
Go
Go.
Bill's father would never knowingly sit down at table with a
    Democrat.
Now Bill says Democracy must go.
Go on Democracy.
Democracy is the shit.
Relativity is the shit.
Dictators are the shit.
Menken is the shit.
Waldo Frank is the shit.
The Broom is the shit.
Dada is the shit.
Dempsey is the shit.
This is not a complete list.
They say Ezra is the shit.
But Ezra is nice.

Come let us build a monument to Ezra.
Good a very nice monument.
You did that nicely.
Can you do another?
Let me try and do one.
Let us all try and do one.
Let the little girl over there on the corner try and do one.
Come on little girl.
Do one for Ezra.
Good.
You have all been successful children.
Now let us clean the mess up.
The Dial does a monument to Proust.
We have done a monument to Ezra.
A monument is a monument.
After all it is the spirit of the thing that counts.

Paris, 1923
Querschnitt (Autumn 1924)

58 Part Two of the Soul of Spain with McAlmon and Bird the Publishers.

You come to Spain but do not remain. Anna Veronica, Marcial Veronica, Pablo Veronica, Gitanillo Veronica. No they cannot Veronica because the wind blows. The wind blows and it does not snows look at the bull with his bloody nose.

Part Three of The Soul of Spain with McAlmon and Bird the Publishers.

There is no night life in Spain. They stay up late but they get up late. That is not night life. That is delaying the day. Night life is when you get up with a hangover in the morning. Night life is when everybody says what the hell and you do not remember who paid the bill. Night life goes round and round and you look at the wall to make it stop. Night life comes out of a bottle and goes into a jar. If you think how much are the drinks it is not night life.

Part Four of the Same Story.

After a while there were no bull fights. What the hell no bull fights? No bull fights. Not really you can't mean it no bull fights. But there were no bull fights.

Part Five Follows.

We got on a train and went somewhere else.

Part Six   A Serious and Vivid Account of a Dramatic Moment in the Cruel Sport.

Estocada stuck well stuck. They run round in circles
with the capes and the bull whirls round and round and then
goes down and folds his knees under and his tongue sticks out
and the sword sticks out dully the hilt and the banderillos
stick out sharply at angles. Well stuck by the applauded
diestro. Well stuck by the afamoused espada. They are going
to kill him back of the horns with the short knife.

Short knives are thickshort knives are quick short knives make
a needed nick.

Women love to see the puntillo used. It is exactly like
turning off an electric light bulb.

Paris, 1923
Querschnitt (November 1924)

59 To Chink Whose Trade Is Soldiering

When you are picked up dead
Your face gone ugly tight
The situation clearly outlined
By the dead
We won't believe you're gone
Your boots have dropped too many times
We've drunk too much good beer
Watched the sun rise
And cursed the rain
That spoiled the piste
Or turned the river brown
So flies were useless

Paris, 1924

60 [Some day when you are picked up . . .]

Some day when you are picked up
Stiff
Awkward to carry
The situation clearly outlined by the dead
I will think how we spoke of Ney reported hammering on a
field piece with his broken sword, the statue seen through
the leaves of the trees from the terrace of the Closerie, and
of this thing and that thing which we had seen.
I will remember how you carried my pack over the St.
Bernard.
And the many times we drank together. Drunk on beer.
Drunk on whiskey. Drunk on wine. Drunk many times.
Always happy.
Drunk in Milan at Campari's.
Drunk in Cologne at Werzel's.
Drunk in the mountains
And in the evening before the meal was ready, drinking Irish
whiskey and water. Drunk in Pamplona on absinthe in the
white wicker chairs outside the Suizo. Always talking. Talking
of your trade and my trade and the Empire and people we
knew and bulls and horses, places we had been and plans
and projects and the necessity for money, overdrafts and how
to handle tailors, the Empire again and the great good in
drinking, shooting, and when drunk I boasted and you never
minded. Ireland, you predicted the death of Mick Collins and
of Griffith, Russia and the funny stories of Chicherin.

Paris, 1924

Matisse   Die Odaliske. Zeichnung. (Mit Genehmigung der Marées Ges.)

THE LADY POETS WITH FOOT NOTES
By *ERNEST HEMINGWAY*

One lady poet was a nymphomaniac and wrote for Vanity Fair. [1])

One lady poet's husband was killed in the war. [2])

One lady poet wanted her lover, but was afraid of having a baby. When she finally got married, she found she couldn't have a baby. [3])

One lady poet slept with Bill Reedy got fatter and fatter and made half a million dollars writing bum plays. [4])

One lady poet never had enough to eat. [5])

One lady poet was big and fat and no fool. [6])

---

[1]) College nymphomaniac. Favourite lyric poet of leading editorial writer N. Y. Tribune.

[2]) It sold her stuff.

[3]) Favourite of State University male virgins. Wonderful on unrequited love.

[4]) Stomach's gone bad from liquor. Expects do something really good soon.

[5]) It showed in her work.

[6]) She smoked cigars all right, but her stuff was no good.

61 The Lady Poets With Foot Notes

One lady poet was a nymphomaniac and wrote for Vanity Fair.[1]
One lady poet's husband was killed in the war.[2]
One lady poet wanted her lover, but was afraid of having a
baby. When she finally got married, she found she couldn't
have a baby.[3]
One lady poet slept with Bill Reedy got fatter and fatter
and made half a million dollars writing bum plays.[4]
One lady poet never had enough to eat.[5]
One lady poet was big and fat and no fool.[6]

[1]College nymphomaniac. Favourite lyric poet of leading editorial writer
N.Y. Tribune.
[2]It sold her stuff.
[3]Favourite of State University male virgins. Wonderful on unrequited love.
[4]Stomach's gone bad from liquor. Expects to do something really good
soon.
[5]It showed in her work.
[6]She smoked cigars all right, but her stuff was no good.

Paris, ca. 1924
Querschnitt (November 1924)

62 The Poem Is By Maera

Picture by Juanito Quintana—6 Miuras Pamplona. Before the paseo. Matadors Rodolfo Gaona, Jose Gomez (Gallito), Juan Belmonte—Banderilleros MAERA—Magritas, Almendro. Picture taken just before the paseo. Gaona shows fear. The others show various degrees of contempt.

Poem

Everybody steps
Everybody steps
You will also step
Gaona.

José has always stepped
Juan will always step
You will also step
Gaona.

Magritas steps
Almendro steps
I have always stepped
Gaona.

There are only two
Only two for you
Step along with us
GAONA.

Two are only two
Only two for you
Step along with us
GAONA.

Bulls are only bulls
All of us are men
Step along with us
Gaona.

You can place the sticks
You know all the tricks
Try to be a man
Gaona.

Now it starts to go
Now we have to show
See if you can step
GAONA.

Everybody steps
You will also step
You had better step
Gaona.

Pamplona or Paris, 1925

A Valentine
and
Other
Offerings

1926-1935

Surely goodness and mercy shall
follow me all the days of
my life and I shall
never escape them
Though I walk through the
[shadow] of the shadow
of death I shall return
to do evil.

For thou art with me
In the morning and the evening
Especially in the evening
The wind blows in the [fall]
And it is all over

When I walk through the valley
of the shadow of death —
I shall [fear] all evil
For thou art with me.

The Lord is my shepherd
I shall not want him long
He maketh me to lie down in
green pastures
And there are no green pastures
He leadeth me beside still
waters
And still waters reflect thy face
For thou art with me

In the morning and the evening
And in the night the wind
blows and [thou] art
with me.
You have gone and it is
all gone with you
The wind blows in the fall
and it is all over.
Surely goodness and mercy
shall follow me all the days of
my life and I shall never escape
them. For thou art with me

The Lord is my shepherd
   I shall not want him for long
He maketh me to lie down in green pastures
   and there are no green pastures
He leadeth me beside still waters
   and still waters run deep
the wind blows and the bark of the trees is wet from the r[ain]
the leaves fall and the trees are bare in the [wind fall]
Leaves float on the still waters
There are wet dead leaves in the basin of the fountain

Working drafts, "Neothomist Poem," 192[6]

63 Neothomist Poem

The Lord is my shepherd, I shall not
                     want him for long.

Paris, 1926
Exile (Spring 1927)

64 [And everything the author knows ...]

And everything the author knows
He shows and shows and shows and shows
His underclothes
Are more important than the sun.
A work begun
Means many buttons more undone
The author's wife or wives
Gives me the hife or hives
Some authors write about the poor
Describe the workings of a sewer
Narrate the contents of a drain
All authors give each other pain
Another author writes of riches
His characters all sons of bitches
His women prey to fancy itches
For one another or their brother
Another author loves his mother
Some authors write of happy things
And make much money to drink
themselves to death with and forget
their troubles by inhaling gaseous
champagne bubbles.
Some authors think the things they
write are of importance little
knowing
But ever flowing.

Paris, 1926

65 [I think that I have never trod . . .]

I think that I have never trod
On anything as swell as sod
Sod whose hungry heart extracts
The wisdom of the railway tracks
Sod that underneath thy feets
Produces pumpkins trees and beets
That lies on mother nature's breast
And gives the meadow lark a nest
Trees are made by fools like God
Who pushes them up through the sod.

L'Envoi

For God is love and love is sod
Let all unite to worship God.
And let the Maker's trembling hand
Emulate the ductless gland
Thus are we in His wisdom brought
To see the things that God has wrought.

Paris, 1926
New York Times Magazine (16 October 1977)

66 [Little drops of grain alcohol . . .]

Little drops of grain alcohol
Little slugs of gin
Make the mighty notions
Make the double chin—
Lovely Mrs. Parker in the Algonquin
Loves her good dog Robinson
Keeps away from sin
Mr. Hemingway now wears glasses
Better to see to kiss the critics' asses—

New Verse

Oh it's always fair weather
When Mr. McGregor pulls Mr. Benchley together—

Paris, 1926

67 To a Tragic Poetess

Nothing in her life became her like her almost leaving of it.

Oh thou who with a safety razor blade
a new one to avoid infection
Slit both thy wrists
the scars defy detection
Who over-veronaled to try and peek
into the shade
Of that undistant country from whose bourne
no traveller returns who hasn't been there.
But always vomited in time
and bound your wrists up
To tell how you could see his little hands
already formed
You'd waited months too long
that was the trouble.
But you loved dogs and other people's children
and hated Spain where they are cruel to donkeys.
Hoping the bulls would kill the matadors.
The national tune of Spain was Tea for Two
you said and don't let anyone say Spain to you—
You'd seen it with the Seldes
One Jew, his wife and a consumptive
you sneered your way around
through Aragon, Castille and Andalucia.
Spaniards pinched
the Jewish cheeks of your plump ass
in holy week in Seville
forgetful of our Lord and of His passion.
Returned, your ass intact, to Paris
to write more poems for the New Yorker.
To sit one day in the Luticia
and joke about a funeral passing in the rain
It gave no pain
because you did not know the people.

To celebrate in borrowed cadence
your former gnaw and itch for Charley
who went away and left you not so flat behind him
And it performed so late those little hands
those well formed little hands
And were there little feet and had
the testicles descended?
While in Malaga the street lights in the fog
outside the hospital
A boy named Litri
returning from death's other kingdom to discover
they'd taken off his leg without permission
Having promised it was only to clean the wound
The leg gone at the hip
suffered a *crise* of *desespoir*
desesperado
Knowing before he died of gaseous gangrene
he'd never fight again
It mattered greatly.
He died *desesperado* in his bed as did Maera
Although Maera slipped from bed
to die upon the floor
Curled up under the bed
the tubes in his chest broken
His face quite happy
considering he drowned in mucous
He thinking in delirium he was a boy again and voyaging
under the seats in third class coaches
his fighting cape rolled up to make a pillow.
An old man named Valentin Magarza
climbed in his eightieth year the tower of Miguelete
and was, the Valencian paper said,
destroyed completely on the pavement.
His granddaughter had said he was a bother
and he was getting old.
A boy named Jaime Noain
exploded in his mouth for love

a three inch stick of dynamite
And lived, unknowing, to become
the chief attraction of a troupe
of horrors
who visit all the fairs of Catalonia.
Fifteen a day they average in the papers
The suicides of sunny Spain
the column headed LOS DESESPERADOS
A separate heading sometimes, AHOGADOS
or, The Drowned Ones.
Thus tragic poetesses are made
by observation.

Paris, 1926

68 Portrait of a Lady

[Extract]

Now we will say it with a small poem. A poem that will not
be good. A poem that will be easy to laugh away and will not
mean anything. A mean poem. A poem written by a man with
a grudge. A poem written by a boy who is envious. A poem
written by someone who used to come to dinner. Not a nice
poem. A poem that does not mention the Sitwells. A poem
that has never been in England. A small poem to hurt ones
feelings. A poem in which there are no crows. A poem in
which nobody dies. A small poem that does not say it about
love. A poem written by someone who does not know any
better. A poem that is envious. A poem that is cheap. A poem
that is not worth writing. A poem that why are such poems
written. A poem that is it a poem. A poem that we had better
write. A poem that could be better written. A poem. A poem
that states something that everybody knows. A poem that
states something that people have not thought of. An
insignificant poem. A poem or not.

> Gertrude Stein was never crazy
> Gertrude Stein was very lazy.

Now that it is all over perhaps it made a great difference if it was
something that you cared about.

Paris, ca. 1926

69 Sequel

So if she dies
And if you write of it
Being a writer and a shit
Dulling it so you sleep again at night,
Alone or telling it to whores
Their minds are dull
But oh their cunts are in the proper place
You pay them but sometimes they like it too
And feel your wounds more eagerly than they feel you,

Paris, ca. 1926

70 [The rail ends do not meet . . .]

The rail ends do not meet
The sun goes down
And only rivers run no race
Nor does still water run so deep
Levine, Levine the Hebrew ace
Mackerel skies at night are the sailor's delight
Or they break the sailor's heart
A sailor's life is the life for me
The ground rolls green
As green as the sea

Paris, ca. 1927

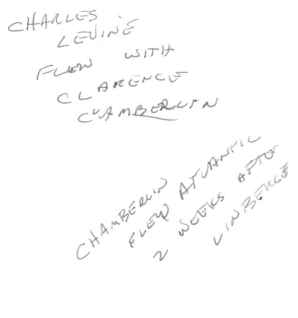

CHARLES
LEVINE
FLEW WITH
CLARENCE
CHAMBERLIN

CHAMBERLIN
FLEW ATLANTIC
2 WEEKS AFTER
LINBERGE

71 Valentine

For a Mr. Lee Wilson Dodd and Any of His Friends
who Want it.

Sing a song of critics
pockets full of lye
four and twenty critics
hope that you will die
hope that you will peter out
hope that you will fail
so they can be the first one
be the first to hail
any happy weakening or sign of quick decay.
(All are very much alike, weariness too great,
sordid small catastrophes, stack the cards on fate,
very vulgar people, annals of the callous,
dope fiends, soldiers, prostitutes,
men without a gallus*)
If you do not like them lads
one thing you can do
stick them up your asses lads
My Valentine to you.

*. . . . .

Paris, ca. 1927
Little Review (May 1929)

They say it's over

The need now is for order, only;
Not for subtlance
and piety in one form or another
our works must lead to something
preferrably ~~very~~ dull and morally instructive
But stemming from the classics
Which mostly dealt, if I remember,
with incest, rapes, and wars
and ~~splendid~~ dirty stories
Ovid for instance and ~~Apuleius~~ Petronius.
A Humanist was once a man
who knew his latin and his greek;
good things to know.
It does no harm to know your French, your German
and your Spanish too,
Though if you do not learn them at an University,
Some boy who went to Princeton
will ~~feel~~ privileged
to speak of you as lacking education.
~~However, we of this so-called generation~~
~~But we~~ of this frankly for a generation
Who have killed other men
Have fought in foreign wars,
Buried our friends,
Buried our fathers
when these ~~who far forgot themselves~~ did shoot themselves for diverse reasons

Working draft, "Poem, 1928," 1929.

72 Poem, 1928

They say it's over
The need, now, is for order,
Not for substance
For piety
We must be full of grace, or on the way there,
Our works must lead to something,
Morally instructive, dull, but stemming from the classics
Which mostly dealt, if I remember,
With incest, rapes, and wars
And dirty stories
My Ovid, James, where is it got to—
But we
Who have killed other men,
Have fought in foreign wars,
Buried our friends,
Buried our fathers, when these did shoot themselves for
    economic reasons—
An American gesture to replace bare bodkins with the Colt or
    Smith and Wesson
Who know our mothers for bitches,
We who have slept with women in different countries
And experienced great pleasures,
Have contracted diseases,
Been cured, married and born children
Who have seen revolutions, counter-revolutions and
Counter-counter-revolutions
Who have seen many systems of government
And many good men murdered
Who have been at Troy
In Flanders in Artois and in Picardy
During the fighting there,
(I speak literally,)
Who have seen an army defeated in Asia Minor
And cast into the sea

Who have lived in other countries as well as our own have
   spoken and understood the language of these countries
   and have heard what was said by the people;
We have something that cannot be taken from us by an article
Nor abolished by a critical agreement of Professors
The searchers for order will find that there is a certain
   discipline in the acceptance of experience.
They may, that is;
They rarely find out anything they cannot read in books or
   articles
But if we last and are not destroyed
And we are durable because we have lasted. We do not destroy
   easily.
We'll write the books.
They will not read them
But their children may
If they have children

                                        Berlin, 1929

73 [Little Mr. Wilson . . .]

Little Mr. Wilson
Wrote a little book
Maxie Perkins published it,
(A friend of Mr. Snook)
No one liked to screw in it
Wilson is pedantic
So if you liked to screw your girl
Chirps Wilson "Too Romantic"
All the ball-less critics
All their cuntless wives
Give to Mr. Hemingway
A violent case of Hives.

Billings, Montana
30 November 1930
New York Times Magazine
(16 October 1977)

Age 31

97

74 Advice to a Son

Never trust a white man,
Never kill a Jew,
Never sign a contract,
Never rent a pew.
Don't enlist in armies;
Nor marry many wives;
Never write for magazines;
Never scratch your hives.
Always put paper on the seat,
Don't believe in wars,
Keep yourself both clean and neat,
Never marry whores.
Never pay a blackmailer,
Never go to law,
Never trust a publisher,
Or you'll sleep on straw.
All your friends will leave you
All your friends will die
So lead a clean and wholesome life
And join them in the sky.

Berlin, 1931
Omnibus: Almanach auf das Jahr 1932

75 Lines to Be Read at the Casting of Scott FitzGerald's Balls into the Sea from Eden Roc (Antibes, Alpes Maritimes)

Whence from these gray
Heights unjockstrapped wholly stewed he
Flung
Himself?
No.
Some waiter?
Yes.
Push tenderly oh green shoots of grass
Tickle not our Fitz's nostrils
Pass
The gray moving unbenfinneyed sea
    depths deeper than our debt to Eliot
Fling flang them flung his own his
    two finally his one
Spherical, colloid, interstitial,
uprising lost to sight
in fright
natural
not artificial
no ripples make as sinking sanking
    sonking sunk

Key West, 1935

99

Farewells

1944-1956

76 First Poem to Mary in London

I loving only the word
Trying to make with a phrase and a sentence
Something no bomber can reach
Something to stand when all of us are gone
And long after:
(Given a little luck at the moment of wording)
(Needing much luck then. Playing it out when I get it)
    Come now to a new city.
(Owning no part of it. Shy from too long on the water. Killing
I know and believe in. Or do not believe in but practice.
Practice make perfect make practice make perfect make
practice. People I cannot explain to. Eyes burned from the
sun on the water. My heart, my dear, was eaten by a
trunkback turtle who did not recognize the taste and all my
hopes are part of a shoal where the Red Groupers spawned a
month ago.)
    Now come to this city tired and shy and living with my true
headache who is faithful and true and never leaves me. My
headache never had a brother before and so he does not
know that they become tired. He does not know that all of us
need to be alone. He is a friendly and true headache and I do
not like him to know that he bores me.
    Only in the air does he leave me. Selfishly shifting the
ear-phones, I am unfaithful a little. The days between flying
are months. And a week between flying is always. But never
let my headache know because I should not wish to hurt his
feelings.
    Sitting now here in the room waiting to go to the battle. A man
without his children nor his cats. No mangoes growing in the
ante-room of the Dorchester and the five inch bath instead of the
long plunge into the differing temperatures of the pool in Sum-
mer. His boat is in the far away sea. His people are dispersed
and his armament surrendered to the proper authorities. Duly re-
ceipted and accounted for.

The battle will be another man's battle and we will only be baggage. Sharing a jeep with three others. Your choice between drunkards or liars.

No, it is not a good ending. Not the end we had hoped for. Not as when sighting her rising we closed dry mouthed but happy. Not as we thought it would be in the long nights on the bridge with the head-phones. Not as we thought it should be each time we took her from harbour.

Where are you Wolfie now? Where are you Paxtchi? Put her on the fucking course. Who gives a shit for these bastards? Not us, we know, and always tried to close and have that now the only wealth that we will ever keep. But you can't spend that here in this hotel. And if you could I'd starve before I'd eat on it or drink on it and I can't even go to see the censor because of changes that are made; not in the copy but in me.

Then I am homesick for Paxtchi who took the armour from his cockpit so she would trim better in the sea and never dropped the drums of gas he sat on when we closed. For Wolfie standing on the flying bridge the muscles jumping in his cheeks. Saying, "Papa it's all right with me. Don't worry for a moment Papa it's all right with me."

So now I sit in this town, homesick and lonely for the sea. By-passing the town while I am in it. Taking what pleasure I meet but sick and alone for the sea and my people. The headache does not matter. I have good fun with the mob and have not become a sad one. Don't worry Wolfie. Never. It is all right. I promise you always it is all right.

For in the evening now, alone from choice, I watch the clock electrically tick and jump forward toward the hour when she will come opening softly with the in-left key. Saying "May I come in?" Coming small-voiced and lovely to the hand and eye to bring your heart back that was gone; to cure all loneliness and bring the things we left behind upon the boat.

Don't worry Wolfie, ever. I'm all right and would not change for any ever time. We've taken losses and we've made great gains and nothing ever bores us when it starts. Not even someone else's battle.

(I'll write you more about this later)

London, May 1944
Atlantic (August 1965)

Poem To Mary. (Second Poem)

Now sleeps he
With that old whore death
Who, yesterday, denied her thrice

Repeat after me

Now sleeps he
With that old whore death
Who, yesterday, denied her thrice.
Pause. Wait for them to close up.
Continue.
Do you take this old whore

death for thy lawful
wedded wife

Repeat after me

I do

I do

(margin, left side, rotated): Did you deny her? You? Thrice?
Repeat after me

(top marginal note): insert where it says (sweet christmas) on page ⑧

Christmas Feast *(crossed out)*

All of us will Die today
Hail To Father christmas
Old and young Together Say
Hail To Father Christmas
Bright the Colored Flash Spits Shining
Hail to Father christmas
Bright today our love Divine
Hail To Father Christmas.
Come let's Put it on the line
Hail To Father christmas
It is No Longer christmas

and from this hill, bare-topped, its
flanks covered with christmas trees
many further hills are seens

(right margin, rotated): Plus one of the following @ christmas never ending Then The line ③ Hail To Faith christmas

77 Poem to Mary (Second Poem)

Now sleeps he
With that old whore Death
Who, yesterday, denied her thrice.
Repeat after me
Now sleeps he
With that old whore Death
Who, yesterday, denied her thrice.
Pause. Wait for them to close up.
Continue.
Did you deny her?
Yes.
Thrice?
Yes.
Repeat after me.
Do you take this old whore
Death for thy lawful
Wedded wife?
Repeat after me
I do
I do
I do.
K.I.A. 6 off. 61 em. 13 Sept. 2400—14 Sept. 2400.
Translate
Killed in action 6 officers 61 enlisted men from midnight 13th
    September to midnight 14th September
Repeat after me sixtyseven times
I do
I do
I do, sixtyseven times
Continue
It is continued
In the next war we shall bury the dead in cellophane
In the next war we shall bury the dead in cellophane
The Host shall come packaged in every K ration

107

"Poem to Mary (Second Poem)," 1944.

The Host shall come packaged in every K ration

Every man shall be provided with a small but perfect
  Archbishop Spellman, which shall be self-inflatable (courtesy
  of Air Reduction, opened—closed—previous—opened—
  closed—)

You don't need to repeat this. There is not any ceremony any
  more.

Everyone is gone and you say this out loud to yourself.

You are alone at the time and the time now is always. Always was
  a word you used in promises. It is valueless.

All officers, warrant officers and enlisted men will be
  provided with a copy of their own true loves that they will
  never see again and all these copies will be returnable
  through the proper channels.

My own true love is Mary Welsh.

Then, of course, she will be returnable.

But I, on this day, will not accept the signature of Archbishop
  Spellman. Nor of you. Nor of you. Nor of you.

You may all go now, all of you. Go as quietly as possible.
  Go as far as possible. You may even take possible with you
  if you can find him. And you may hang him or dispose of
  him in any manner that you see fit.

Today no one uses slang because clarity is of the utmost
  importance.

Fucking, alone, is retained, but is only used as an adjective.

Sweating out is retained.

It means that which one must suffer without any possibility of
  changing the result or the outcome.

Those of us who know walk very slowly, and we look at one
  another with infinite love and compassion.

This comes only after one hundred days and is one of the
  final symptoms.

There has been irritation, anger, fear, doubt, accusations,
  denials, misinterpretations, mistakes, cowardice, inability and
  lack of talent for this work.

All this has been and will be again. To be counterbalanced

by firmness, steadiness, courage, quick understanding and the ability both to maneuver and to fight.

But now, for a moment, there is only love and compassion. Know how to endure. And only love and compassion.

Repeat it.

Only love and compassion.

For the B.F.'s too?

(Battle Fatigues, officers, men, midnight 13th Sept _____? midnight 14th Sept.)

No.

Then it is not compassion.

Not for the B.F.'s too. And

Yes, it is love and compassion.

How can you say that here?

How can you say the other?

Not that we ask for more. Not that we wish ever any. Not that we wish any all. Not that we want any greater.

But when they walked away from that undiscovered country from whose bourne no traveller returns who hasn't been there,

They walked away from this we cannot state. And in them died this inner knowing that grows—fresher and lovelier than any rose. Manured by death and watered only with unshed tears until, this day, it flowers into this love and this compassion.

Not for them.

No. I am sorry.

Then it is not complete.

No, nor will it be ever.

There is no contrition.

(No bloody fucking contrition)

Only love and compassion.

Reach out your hand to Love's dark sister Hate, and walk with her across that hill we slowly walked, and see if Love is waiting at the top. Or who is waiting there instead.

Did I tell you my heart is a target of opportunity?

Love's lovely sister
Lovingly unloving
Unworryingly succeeding
Procuring unprocuringly
Never wholly wrong
Nor more than half right
Holding unholdingly to hold where Love leaves easily without address.
Love lightly leaves without a trace and her dark sister fills in all the forms
All all the forms so neatly filled
The writing clear and good, where Love's is often quite illegible
Scrawled lightly in a hurry as she smiled,
Giving unimportance to the page.
Do you think there upon the hill, we'll find her there?
No. She's long gone. She never stands to fight.
Knowing too well the idiocy of battle, Love's always gone, leaving us only the deserted sacrament
As one finds dinner on the table in the house of a new taken village.
So that we wear it now. Traces of it are worn on our chins. Like remnants of the yolk of the rare and much desired egg, our scooped up, newly eaten sacrament.
Bringing it with our newly issued pictures of our true loves up toward the high ground beyond the town. Up toward the easy, dirt-mouthed smile we had denied so many days (D plus 108)
Now all move slowly plodding up that hill
Making feet slowly go where they know better than to take you.
Feet are wise and feet are wary
Feet of John and feet of Harry
Feet know better
Feet won't go.
Make feet move on slowly now
Make feet follow where no plow
Leads you ahead
Where things are sown

Toward the place where you'll be dead.
RETURN HER NOW THROUGH THE PRESCRIBED CHANNELS.
   RETURN HER.
This will aid you.
      Song to Aid You to Return Her.
"What they will do to others,
"They will do to you.
"If you never suffer
"God will see you through.
"Onward Christian soldiers
"Marching to a whore
"With the cross of Mary Welsh
"Going on before.
   (Throw your love away)
You must do it slowly now
"Slowly now and pray
"Pray to all of nothing
"Pray to all of nil
"Throw away your own true love
"Walking up a hill."
Repeat it now again:
Now sleeps he
With that old whore Death
Who, yesterday, denied her thrice.
If you know, if you conceive
If you too. If. If. If. (Not the poem that was given you framed for
   Christmas in Oak Park, Illinois, written by Rudyard Kipling.)
But the other If.
Older than the If of Hamlet.
The old long ugly If that we have faced
In all the nights and all the forests of our hearts,
Always coming out into a clearing
Always sighting finally the smoke of the camp fire.
Now on this wooded hill again
If iffingly to proceed
If me no ifs, my true love

While we expend that which is not expendable,
While we violate all that is inviolate,
While we destroy that which is indestructable.
With nothing more than harrassing fire.
Nothing more than that.
All my heart is a target of opportunity,
All of us have been interdicted.
This is not the way it was.
I have not been there.
No one was there.
No one saw it.
Your guess is as good as mine.
Make a guess now while it is easy.
Get your guess in early.
Try and get your guess in for tonight, especially for tonight.
Tonight would be bank night for Archbishop Spellman.
If we were catholics.
And there are only 89 more days until Christmas (put in Xmas)
All of us will die today
Hail to Father Christmas
Old and young together say,
Hail to Father Christmas
Bright the colored flack spits shine
Hail to Father Christmas.
Bright today our love divine
Hail to Father Christmas.
D plus one O one O nine
Hail to Father Christmas.
Christmas minus ninety-nine
Hail to Father Christmas
Come, let's put it on the line,
Hail to *Fa-a-a-ther* Christmas

It is no longer Christmas
And from this hill, bare-topped,
Its flanks covered with Christmas trees,
Many further hills are seen.

So, Mary, now I love you straight and true and send you this to let you know that we had a rather sticky day today in the forest. Casualties were fairly heavy, and a certain amount of battle fatigue. Many more than there should be. But there are many contributing factors. I'm getting sort of mixed up on a lot of things again. But much clearer on others. Very hard to write about this stuff. It is different from the boat. In the boat we were always waiting for it. Here it is the happening all the time and who it happens to. I do not think about me at all any more. Bragging again. I think about you and that brings me in. I write you awfully dull letters darling, because I get tired and sort of emptied out. And all I have to tell you that I can write is that I love you.

ERNEST

Paris, September-October 1944
Atlantic (August 1965)

78 Poetry

So now,
Loseing the three last night,
Takeing them back today,
Dripping and dark the woods . . .

Buchet, France, 24 September 1944
How It Was (1976)

79 Defense of Luxembourg

So now,
  Alive
John Daughty Dead
    The chutes hanging from the trees
    And the high tension wires
All of us long gone
  Firing on all airplanes
  Unbelieving nothing
  Nor his brother
  Except that we attack at first light
Come now and join us.
  Bring for the week end
  Ability to read a map
  (This corresponds to shaving kit and pyjamas)
Bring Unfear of death
  (This corresponds to the formerly seven now five packs of
  nationally advertised brands issued at the PX with cheerful
  banter in the basement of the Scribe)
Bring knowledge, subtlety, side-slippering, hardiness, fortitude,
  quick and sound decisions, and the ability to abandon
  knowingly and soundly all hope of every kind yet stay and
  fight.
  (This corresponds to a present to your hostess; a trifle
  well selected with semi-impeccable taste)
Bring fuck-all,
Bring worthless
Bring no-good—
They can be carried as banners.
Or in the pocket.
But bring them to where we go now.
They are as valuable as soap (soap is made from the dead
horses of horse cavalrymen's dreams) and there is
No need to bring money.
No one can change it.

Bring shit
Bring Fuck
Bring hatred of these cocksuckers.
Now it starts to roll as when the wind comes into the trees in
  a forest fire
Come on let's go.
What the fuck is holding it up.
What the fuck is holding you up
It beats the shit out of me Lieutenant
Let's go
White jumped off at 0840
They are held up by M.G. fire. Krauts
are infiltrating behind our lines. We are fighting them now.
S6 states he wants to jump-off regardless. Blue following will
mop up infiltrated enemy.
Let's go.

Finca Vigia, Cuba, 1945

①

Defense of Luxembourg

So now,

alive
John Daughty Dead.

The chutes hanging from the trees.

And the high tension wires

all of us long gone

Firing on all air-planes

an unbelieving noting

Nor his brother

Except that we _____ at burst light

Come now and join us.

Bring for the week end

ability to read a map

(This corresponds to shaving kit and py jamas).

Bring unfear of death

(This corresponds to the formerly seen now

 _____ packs of _____ _____ issued PX
Tooth brush and the PX-ed (tooth paste
 advertised brands usual _____ PX _____ _____
 _____ in the basement _____ _____ PX _____ _____

Working draft, "Defense of Luxembourg," 1945.

80 To Crazy Christian

There was a cat named Crazy Christian
Who never lived long enough to screw
He was gay hearted, young and handsome
And all the secrets of life he knew
He would always arrive on time for breakfast
Scamper on your feet and chase the ball
He was faster than any polo pony
He never worried a minute at all
His tail was a plume that scampered with him
He was black as night and as fast as light.
So the bad cats killed him in the fall.

Finca Vigia, Cuba, ca. 1946

81   Poem to Miss Mary

Now, Mary, you can face it good
And face it in your widow-hood
That where we've gone we've always been
So all the things that we have seen
The brown, the yellow and the green
Were small, and big and un-precise
Or very clear and quite precise
But they were very, very nice,
And crawled on us like country lice,
Until we rolled them off with dice.
They came from anywhere.
Now anywhere's a lovely place
For members of the human race, in which race,
IF your dues are paid
You carry, always, your own spade.
A spade is good and kind and sweet
Yet it can cut sufficient deep.
So sleep well, darling.
Sleep well, please,
And know that I am at my ease.

                    Paris, 26 November 1949

82   Across the Board

The thudding was inaudible
And when they jumped it made no sound.
Papa, it's Richard, the tall boy said.
I knew him when he turned his head
But everything inside was dead.
We put the calva in the wound;
It had all orchards in the rain,
To ease our old and modern pain.
But light she was and light for me
And who slept with eternity?
Eternity is scarcely found
Until we're underneath the ground
Where thudding hooves will seldom sound.
Perhaps they will,
I do not know;
Let's play to win and place and show.

Paris, December 1949

83 Black-Ass Poem After Talking to Pamela Churchill

We leave them all quite easily
When dislike overcomes our love.
Though nothing is done easily
When there's been love.
We leave and go and go to where?
What treasures are entrusted there?
Who knows when treasures treasures are
Who's only seen them from afar?
Who, knowing treasure, does not fear
When he has seen it close and near?
Fear not, hie on, close up my lad
That all of gladness may be sad.

Paris, 20 December 1949

84 The Road to Avallon

The negro rich are nigger rich
Upon the road to Avallon—
Wild natural mink is on their backs,
Their shoulders, sleeves, and on their flanks
Once it has grown there is no thanks
So come along.
Nor criticize nor touch the brake
For confidence you must not shake.
You bastard, cur and kindred words
Assembled like some poor dog's turds
To speed you on your way.
Dogs must shit as well as men
I like dogs better
Say: Amen.

Paris, 22 December 1949

85 Country Poem with Little Country

When gin is gone and all is over
Then horses, bees and alsyke clover
Receive our sorrows and our joys:
Be known as well to all our boys
Without much noise.
The noises horses make are good
On turf on sandy roads and wood
The bee recedes and enters fast
He knows the role for which he's cast
The fighter-bomber lives forever
More truly when they're two together
But left wing shortages occur
Who, on the line, called
A dog a cur?

Paris, 22 December 1949

86 Travel Poem

Go Mary I would say to thee
Go everywhere so you might see
Economics and history.
Painting on the walls is found
And no one has to paint his hound
Nor kiss the ass of any king
Nor, know really, anything.
But travel broadens all our parts
The ass first, and at last, our hearts:
If they can take what others made
Knowing it clear in light or shade.
But few have ever learned it so
So go, and throw, and throw and go
Some will catch it off the wall
Others not reach the ball at all.

Paris, 22 December 1949

87 Lines to a Girl 5 Days
After Her 21st Birthday

Back To The Palace
And home to a stone
She travels the fastest
Who travels alone
Back to the pasture
And home to a bone
She travels the fastest
Who travels alone—
Back to all nothing
And back to alone
She travels the fastest
Who travels alone
But never worry, gentlemen
Because there's Harry's Bar
Afderas on The Lido
In a low slung yellow car*
Europeo's publishing
Mondadori doesn't pay
Hate your friends
Love all false things
Some colts are fed on hay
Wake up in the mornings
Venice still is there
Pigeons meet and beg and breed
Where no sun lights the square.
The things that we have loved are in the gray lagoon
All the stones we walked on
Walk on them alone
Live alone and like it
Like it for a day
But I will not *be* alone, angrily she said.

*Translator's note: Mr. H must be insane. They do not have
cars on The Lido.

125

Only in your heart, he said. Only in your head.
But I love to be alone, angrily she said.
Yes, I know, he answered
Yes I know, he said.
But I will be the best one. I will lead the pack.
Sure, of course, I know you will. You have a right to be.
Come back some time and tell me. Come back so I can see.
You and all your troubles. How hard you work each day.
Yes I know he answered.
Please *do* it your own way.
Do it in the mornings when your mind is cold
Do it in the evenings when everything is sold.
Do it in the springtime when springtime isn't there
Do it in the winter
We know winter well
Do it on very hot days
Try doing it in hell.
Trade bed for a pencil
Trade sorrow for a page
No work it out your own way
Have good luck at your age.

Finca Vigia, Cuba, December 1950

88 [If my Valentine you won't be . . .]

If my Valentine you won't be,
I'll hang myself on your Christmas tree.

Finca Vigia, Cuba, 14 February 1956
How It Was (1976)

Explanatory Notes

Related Readings

Acknowledgments

Explanatory Notes

References are to line numbers.

Juvenilia 1912-1917

1. The Opening Game

The manuscript is preserved in Volume IV of Grace Hemingway's family scrapbooks at the John F. Kennedy Library, Boston, Massachusetts.

EH was twelve years old when he wrote this, his first surviving poem, for his mother after he had gone to see his favorite team, the Chicago Cubs, play. Heinie "Zim" Zimmerman appears again in EH's story "The Three-Day Blow."

2—*Chance*: Cubs first baseman Frank Chance.
2—*Evers*: John Evers, Cubs second baseman.
4—*Schulte*: Frank Schulte, Cubs right-fielder.

2. [Blank Verse]

EH's literal rendering of a literary term was originally written to fulfill an English class assignment. It appeared in the "Air Line," the humor column in the school newspaper.

3. Dedicated to F. W.

Title—*F. W.*: Fred Wilcoxen was a classmate and fellow *Trapeze* staffer. The poem is a parody of the seventh stanza of Longfellow's "A Psalm of Life":

> Lives of great men all remind us
> We can make our lives sublime,
> And, departing, leave behind us
> Footprints on the sands of time;

4. How Ballad Writing Affects Our Seniors

5—*Miss Dixon*: Margaret Dixon, one of EH's favorite teachers at Oak Park High School. She and Miss Fannie Biggs were largely responsible for his work in English composition, and, as advisers for the *Tabula*, they accepted his sometimes unorthodox work for publication in the school's literary magazine. See Charles A. Fenton, *The Apprenticeship of Ernest Hemingway*, pp. 6-10.
14—*Lloyd Boyle*: EH's classmate; left high school to go to war.

5. The Worker

Title—Originally titled "The Stoker." In Hemingway's manuscript the poem is set aboard a Great Lakes steamer.

Athletic Verse

Fenton in *Apprenticeship* (p. 20) believed that Fred Wilcoxen was largely responsible for writing these poems, but the surviving manuscript is in EH's hand.

8. The Safety Man

10—*Cole*: Robert Cole, Oak Park High School, class of 1917.

9. The Inexpressible

This poem is modeled on the work of James Whitcomb Riley.

Wanderings 1918-1925

10. The Ship   Translated Being La Paquebot

Written aboard the *Chicago*, the troop ship that carried EH to France. On the third day out of New York, it ran into a storm. The poem is attributed to EH by William Horne and Frederick W. Spiegel who served in Italy with EH.
23—*Fritz the noted Spiegel*: Frederick W. Spiegel.
25—*Captain Pease*: Warren Pease. Member of company of ambulance drivers on board the *Chicago*. Like EH and the others, he was a provisional lieutenant.

11. [There was Ike and Tony and Jaque and me . . .]

The 23-line manuscript of this poem was sold at Sotheby Parke Bernet (25 October 1977, #416). The manuscript has not been located, and the text printed here has been transcribed from the illustration in the sale catalogue.

2—*Schio*: The Italian village northwest of Milan where EH was stationed.

12. A Modern Version of Polonius' Advice

The 28-line manuscript of this poem was sold at Sotheby Parke Bernet (25 October 1977, #415). The manuscript has not been located and the text printed here is taken from the sample included in the catalogue. In *Hamlet* (I, iii) Polonius advises his son on how to conduct himself. EH also parodies Polonius's speech here and in "Advice to a Son" (poem 74).

14. To Will Davies

Title—William Henry Davies. The Welsh-born poet who lived the life of a tramp in England and the United States. After 1905, he began to publish verse based on his experiences. He also wrote auto-biographical prose, including *The Autobiography of a Super-tramp* (1907).

6—*county jail*: As a cub reporter for the *Kansas City Star* in 1917, EH attended executions at the old Jackson County Jail. He used this experience in Chapter XV of *In Our Time*. This poem could have been written in Kansas City; but it was probably written in Chicago in 1920.

14—*Blackstone*: The Blackstone Hotel, Chicago. There is also a less well-known Blackstone Hotel in Kansas City.

18—*Bert Williams*: The black comedian, songwriter, and vaudeville star was a leading performer for the Ziegfeld Follies.

15. The Battle of Copenhagen

This "almost legendary opus . . . this deathless lyric," as Bill Horne called it in a letter to EH (12 December 1929), was composed by EH, Horne, and Y. K. Smith on the roof at 100 Chicago Avenue (see note to poem 26, "Killed   Piave—July 8—1918"). The manuscript had evidently been put away and forgotten for nearly eight years when Horne found it and sent a typed copy to EH in Paris with a letter: "Here it is—in one volume, the works of E. Hemingstein & Horney William, with interpolations by Y. K. Smith. (He did the 'By Hezck,' as I remember it)." This poem is printed from a typescript not typed by EH.

28—*breeks*: Breeches.

40—*plaidies*: Plaids.

56-58—*A half a million Jews . . . Battle of Copenhagen*: Many years after this poem was written, lost, discovered, then mostly forgotten, EH wrote to Fenton on 2 August 1952: "of that great poem which begins A Hundred Thousand Jews Ran Back To Tell The News of The Battle Of Copenhagen. This is not anti-Semitic. It only describes the manner in which information is sometimes received." Mary Hemingway remembers him reciting this poem to her.

17. Captives

The nightmarish setting for this poem seems to be a P.O.W. march in Northern Italy during World War I; however, Fenton claims that it is Thrace during the Greek evacuation (*Apprenticeship*, p. 284).

18. Champs d'Honneur

The following paragraphs were never published with "Champs d'Honneur"; however, in two working drafts, (a) headed "Battle," and (b) headed "Heroes," the poem is preceded by a paragraph; paragraph (c) appears by itself on a separate typescript.

a) **Battle**

War correspondents wrote on their typewriters that a sergeant of marines said, "Come on you sons of bitches do you want to live forever? After which I suppose the men died gladly. But I saw tired soldiers burying dead soldiers and two of the tired ones carried one of the dead ones and they said, "Jesus Christ this bastard's heavy!"

-//-

b) **Heroes**

Some shit heel correspondent with a green brassard wrote
that our top-kick hollered, "Come on you sons of bitches
do you want to live forever?" Top-kick, my ass, the top-kick
was so god-damned scared that he was pissing in his pants if
he wasn't praying.

-//-

c)   They say a sergeant of Marines said, "Come on you sons
of bitches do you want to live forever!" After which, I
suppose, the men died gladly. But I, me, I saw tired soldiers
burying dead soldiers and two of the tired ones lifted a big
one of the dead ones and they said "Jesus Christ this
bastard's heavy

"Do you want to live forever?" became a heroic catch phrase in
World War I; EH probably knew Carl Sandburg's 1920 poem
"Losers," which used the same anecdote about a Marine sergeant.
    The earliest manuscript of the poem is written on paper which
carries the address of the *Cooperative Commonwealth*; EH worked
for the magazine in 1920-1921 while living in Chicago.
Title—*Champs d'Honneur*: Fields of Honor (French).
8—*Choking through the whole attack*: A reference to the gas
warfare of World War I.

19. D'Annunzio

Title—Gabriele D'Annunzio, Italian aristocrat, soldier, author, and pa-
triot. His heroic attitudes about the war caused EH to think that he was
"a little insane," but D'Annunzio was also "a divinely brave swashbuck-
ler." See "Mussolini: Biggest Bluff in Europe," collected in *By-Line*, pp.
61–65; see also *Across the River and Into the Trees*, pp. 49–52.

20. [God is away for the summer . . .]

1—*The Reverend John Timothy Stone*: Minister of the Fourth
Presbyterian Church of Chicago from 1909 to 1930.
11—*the Star and Garter*: Chicago burlesque house.

24. Lines to a Young Lady on Her Having Very Nearly Won a Vögel

Title—*Vögel*: Bird (German).

25. Chapter Heading

After it appeared in *Poetry*, the Irish writer L. A. G. Strong selected this poem for *Best Poems of 1923* (Boston: Small, Maynard, 1924), marking the first appearance of a work by EH in a book published in the United States.

1—*longer thoughts*: A reference to Longfellow's "My Lost Youth":

> "A boy's will is the wind's will,
> And the thoughts of youth are long, long thoughts."

26. Killed   Piave—July 8—1918

EH wrote many of his early poems in 1920-1921 while he was living at Y. K. Smith's apartment at 100 Chicago Avenue and working for the *Cooperative Commonwealth*. Smith's home was a literary salon of sorts; during the evenings friends would gather there and discuss theories of art and literature. EH eluded these discussions and spent much of the time in his room writing. He was present, however, when the atmosphere was more festive, or when a particularly interesting guest like Sherwood Anderson was there. Y. K. Smith's sister, Katy, invited her friend Hadley Richardson to visit from St. Louis. On 21 July 1921 Hadley sent EH a Corona typewriter for his twenty-second birthday. Three days later, she received a group of typed poems. One, "Mitrailliatrice," was written in honor of the Corona. Hadley was moved by a poem called "Desire," which appears here under its later title "Killed   Piave—July 8—1918." Hadley quickly responded, saying that she was "absolutely wild" about these new poems and "Lines to a Young Lady on Her Having Very Nearly Won a Vögel." In her letter Hadley makes a vague reference to "Dial," and in an earlier letter, postmarked 20 July 1921, Hadley had also mentioned "Dial." EH may have submitted some of these poems to the *Dial*.

In 1923, after EH and Hadley had moved to Paris, Ezra Pound submitted some of EH's poetry to Scofield Thayer, the editor of the *Dial*. In the midst of a disagreement with Pound over another submission, T. S. Eliot's "The Waste Land," Thayer brusquely rejected EH's poems. After this, EH took a great deal of pleasure in maligning the *Dial* and particularly its managing editor, Gilbert Seldes, along with Scofield Thayer. Since it seems that Seldes had nothing to do with the poems that Pound submitted to Thayer, there has been some confusion over why EH chose Seldes as a target.

28. Mitrailliatrice

Title—There has been considerable confusion over the spelling of EH's title. It correctly appeared as "Mitrailliatrice" in *Poetry*; however, *Three Stories & Ten Poems* printed it as "Mitraigliatrice." In French the term means machine gun fire.
6—*Corona*: The typewriter that Hadley had sent to EH for his birthday.
7—*mitrailleuse*: Machine gun (French).

29. [On Weddynge Gyftes]

Title—EH wrote a satirical article based on his wedding experiences for the *Toronto Star Weekly*. The short poem served as a prologue to the essay.

30. Ultimately

"Ultimately" was EH's first adult poem to be published in the United States; it appeared in the *Double-Dealer*, a New Orleans magazine, in June 1922. "Ultimately" appeared on the same page as "Portrait," a poem by William Faulkner. It is quite possible—indeed probable—that both of these young writers had their work accepted by the *Double-Dealer* through the influence of Sherwood Anderson. Because of this chance relationship of the two authors' verse, Paul Romaine, a Milwaukee bookseller, asked EH, in 1932, if he could include "Ultimately" in a collection of Faulkner's early poems, *Salmagundi* (Milwaukee: Casanova Press, 1932). Actually, Romaine did not want to put the poem *in* Faulkner's book—he wanted it for the back cover. EH agreed and wrote to his bibliographer, Louis Henry Cohn, that the poem was good enough to be published alongside Faulkner's "early shit" (Baker, *Hemingway Life*, p. 227).

32. ["Blood is thicker than water . . ."]

Title—When EH quarreled with Y. K. Smith, his brother Bill—who had been EH's close friend from boyhood days in Michigan—sided with Y. K., writing to EH in Paris that "Blood is thicker than water." EH then sent this poem to Bill Smith.
4—*a drooling old bitch*: Bill Smith's aunt, Mrs. Joseph William Charles (see Baker, *Hemingway Life*, p. 88).

36. Roosevelt

Title—The poem refers to Theodore Roosevelt.
7—*He could have died*: This line was omitted from *Poetry*.

37. Riparto d'Assalto

Title—*Riparto d'Assalto*: Storm troops (Italian); literally, an attack division.
2—*camion*: A truck or wagon.
10—*Arditi*: Italian shock troops.

38. To Good Guys Dead

The words and phrases that EH lists were common battle cries by English and American "patriots," most of whom never saw the front. In *A Farewell to Arms* Frederic Henry ruminates: "Abstract words such as glory, honor, courage, or hallow were obscene beside the concrete names of villages . . ." (p. 196).

39. [Arsiero, Asiago . . .]

1, 5—*Arsiero, Asiago, Monte Grappa, Monte Corno*: Italian mountain villages and scenes of some of the heaviest fighting between Italian and Austrian troops.

40. Montparnasse

Title—The Left Bank section of Paris where many expatriate artists, writers, and Bohemians lived during the 1920s. See "American Bohemians in Paris," *Toronto Star Weekly* (25 March 1922), collected in *By-Line: Ernest Hemingway*, p. 23.
6—*the Dome*: A popular café in Montparnasse. It is the setting for

some of the early scenes in *The Sun Also Rises* and for sketches in *A Moveable Feast*.

41. Along With Youth

Title—This was also the working title of EH's abandoned novel.
1—*porcupine skin*: During the summer of 1913, at Walloon Lake, Dr. Hemingway made young EH and his friend Harold Sampson eat a porcupine after the two boys had needlessly killed the animal.
4-7—*Stuffed horned owl . . . Chuck-wills-widow*: EH was fond of birds, especially owls, and Dr. Hemingway was an amateur taxidermist.
13—*Tribune*: The *Chicago Tribune*.
17—*the hotel*: The Mansion House, Seney, Michigan. See the opening paragraph of "Big Two-Hearted River."

42. The Earnest Liberal's Lament

"The Earnest Liberal's Lament" achieved a certain notoriety among the New York literary set. At a party that Harold Loeb attended for the staff and friends of the *Broom*, Allen Tate read the poem and the group merrily chimed in as a chorus for the lamenting last two lines. See Harold Loeb, *The Way It Was* (New York: Criterion, 1959), p. 242.
Title—*Earnest*: In a typescript of this poem EH has a footnote in which he dedicates the work to "Noel Buxton, Bertrand Russel, Oswald Garrison Villard." Edward Noel-Buxton was a liberal British statesman and author of several books on the Balkans. Betrand Russell was an English philosopher and pacifist. Oswald Garrison Villard was the editor and president of the *New York Evening Post* and later editor and owner of the *Nation*.

43. The Age Demanded

Title—The title and the rhythm are borrowed from the second part of Ezra Pound's "Hugh Selwyn Mauberly":

> The age demanded an image
> Of its accelerated grimace,
> Something for the modern stage,
> Not, at any rate, an Attic grace;

7-8—*And in the end . . . that it demanded*: An earlier typescript conveyed quite a different effect, with the last two lines reading:

> Yet I don't think the age demanded
> One half the stuff that it was handed.

44. Kipling

Although EH often spoofed Kipling's work, the old Imperialist was an important writer in his eyes; and EH recommended Kipling's stories as necessary reading for anyone who wanted to write.
L'Envoi: EH was fond of using this device he had acquired from Kipling and later from Pound.
1-3—These first three lines are a loose parody of Kipling's "Mandalay."
4—*Harold's*: Possibly Harold Acton; EH ridiculed the effeminate author of *Memoirs of an Aesthete* (1948) in the first chapter of *A Moveable Feast*.

45. Stevenson

This poem is a play on the lines from Robert Louis Stevenson's poem "Requiem":

> Under the wide and starry sky
>   Dig the grave and let me lie.
> Glad did I live and gladly die,
>   And I laid me down with a will.

46. Robert Graves

This is a parody of Robert Graves's "Strong Beer," from *Faeries and Fusiliers* (1917):

> Crags for the mountaineer,
> Flags for the Fusilier,
> For all good fellows, beer!
> Strong beer for me!

But the poem also suggests a subtle distinction between the two World War I veterans, both of whom had been wounded. In his poetry Graves minimizes the horror of war, choosing instead to apply irony to his poetic persona. EH leaves the theatrically absurd elements of war to the English poets who can still laugh about it.

1—*the financier*: Probably Horatio Bottomley, the English financier, patriot, politician, and publisher whom EH later likened to Mussolini in "Mussolini: Biggest Bluff in Europe," *Toronto Daily Star* (27 January 1923), collected in *By-Line*, p. 65.

51. Schwarzwald

Title—*Schwarzwald*: The Black Forest of Germany. See "German Inn-Keepers," *Toronto Daily Star* (5 September 1922), collected in *By-Line*, pp. 36-40.

52. They All Made Peace—What Is Peace?

Two influences should be noted here. First, the poem is written in the style of Gertrude Stein. Second, at the Lausanne Peace Conference EH met William Bolitho Ryall, the representative for the *Manchester Guardian*. EH wrote of Bolitho—as he was known—in 1935: "As I was a kid then, he told me things that were the beginning of whatever education I received in international politics." See "The Malady of Power," *Esquire* (November 1935), collected in *By-Line*, p. 222.

In late 1922, EH covered the war between Greece and Turkey for the *Toronto Daily Star*. A few weeks after witnessing the Greek retreat from Thrace and the evacuation of Smyrna—scenes which, he later claimed, taught him what war was all about—he was sent to the Lausanne Peace Conference. In Asia Minor EH had seen the victims; at Lausanne he saw the "peace makers." In a letter to Edmund Wilson in 1923, he wrote: "The thing in L. R. was a joke. I wrote it in the wagon-restaurant going back to Lausanne, had been at a very fine lunch at Gertrude Stein's and talked there all afternoon and read a lot of her new stuff and then drank a big bottle of Beaune myself in the dining car. Facing opening the wire again in the morning I tried to analyse the conference.

Her method is invaluable for analysing anything or making notes on a person or a place" (Edmund Wilson, *The Shores of Light* [New York: Farrar, Straus and Young, 1952], p. 118).

The poem is a distillation of an event. Louis Zukofsky saw it as such when he served as guest editor of the February 1931 issue of

Poetry. In his manifesto "Program: 'Objectivists' 1931" (pp. 268-272), Zukofsky established some of the qualifications for what constituted "objectivist" literature. Then, as an example of the kind of poetry he was calling for, Zukofsky reprinted EH's poem with the following introduction: "Ernest Hemingway's *They All Made Peace—What Is Peace?* is as good now as it was in *The Little Review* in 1922."

The only humanizing qualities about the delegates are from allusions to funny stories about them that the journalists told to amuse themselves. As in other satirical works, EH relies on a series of clipped characterizations and a linking of odd images to achieve his humor.

1—*Ismet Pasha*: Turkish general. EH thought he looked like "an Armenian lace salesman." One night, at the Palace Hotel bar, some journalists elected EH to go over to Pasha's bodyguard and present him with an exploding cigar. EH approached the armed man and offered him the cigar. In exchange the bodyguard offered EH a Turkish cigarette. When the cigar went off the bodyguard "drew all four pistols at once." See Baker, *Hemingway Life*, pp. 102-103 and "The Malady of Power," *By-Line*, pp. 221-228.

4—*Lord Curzon*: The British delegate who ran the conference by secret diplomacy and high-pressure tactics. Journalists were given his official announcements in daily press releases.

5—*Chicherin*: George Chicherin (Tchitcherin), Soviet Foreign Minister and the only important delegate at Lausanne who held press conferences. See Fenton, *Apprenticeship*, pp. 189-202; "Mussolini: Biggest Bluff in Europe"; and "A Russian Toy Soldier," *Toronto Daily Star* (10 February 1923), collected in *By-Line*, pp. 66-69.

6—*Mustapha Kemal*: Turkish leader of the military rout of the Greeks and founder of the modern Turkish state.

14—*Baron Hayashi*: Japanese delegate Senjuro Hayashi, who later was responsible for the Japanese invasion of Manchuria.

15—*Monsieur Barrère*: Camille Eugene Pierre Barrère, French delegate to the conference.

15—*Marquis Garroni*: The Italian delegate received his instructions directly from Mussolini, who made a personal appearance at the conference.

17-18—*has his picture . . . book upside down*: Mussolini held a news conference when he arrived at Lausanne. When the journalists arrived they found him sitting behind a desk reading a book. "I tip-toed over behind him to see what the book was he was reading with such avid interest," wrote EH. "It was a French-English dictionary—held upside down." See "Mussolini: Biggest Bluff in Europe."

19—*Daily Mail*: The London newspaper which championed Mussolini. EH wrote in the *Star*: "There is something wrong, even histrionically, with a man who wears white spats with a black shirt." See "Mussolini: Biggest Bluff in Europe."

31—*M. Stambuliski*: Premier Alexander Stambuliski of Bulgaria.

32—*M. Venizelos*: Greek ambassador and former premier, Eleutherios Venizelos.

36-37—*Senator Beveridge*: U.S. Senator and author Albert J. Beveridge, who was considered "pro-German" before America's entry into World War I and after the war opposed U.S. participation in the League of Nations.

38—*You know me Al*: EH echoes the title of Ring Lardner's 1916 volume of stories.

39—*Lincoln Steffens*: The muckraking journalist was also present at Lausanne. He saw a great deal of EH there and read some of his short stories in manuscript. Steffens became an early believer in EH's talent and future.

40—*Mosul*: The key city in the oil-producing region along the southeastern border of Turkey. Control of this city (and the oil) was a great point of controversy between the British and the Turks; finally, in 1926, Britain managed to have Mosul declared to be within the border of Iraq, which was under British mandate.

41—*The Greek Patriarch*: In August 1921, the Metropolitan of the Greek Orthodox Church of Smyrna was hanged by the Turks.

53. I Like Americans

By-Line—*By A Foreigner*: EH's by-line did not appear when "I Like Americans" and "I Like Canadians" were published in the *Toronto Star Weekly*. These poems are attributed to EH on the basis of manuscripts at the Kennedy Library that EH signed "By a Foreigner." Furthermore, these poems bear a stylistic resemblance to "The Big Dance on the Hill" and "The Sport of Kings," both by EH.

19—*Bill Bryan*: William Jennings Bryan.

20—*Billy Sunday*: American evangelist and proponent of Prohibition.

24—*Barney Google, Mutt and Jeff*: Comic strip characters.
25—*Jiggs*: The husband in the comic strip "Bringing Up Father."

54. I Like Canadians

19—*Woodbine*: A Toronto racetrack.
20—*Blue Bonnets*: A Montreal racetrack.

57. The Soul of Spain with McAlmon and Bird the Publishers

"The Soul of Spain" is loosely based on EH's first trip to Spain in 1923, and it reflects Gertrude Stein's influence—her use of repetition and eccentric syntax—on EH's writing.
Title—*McAlmon*: Robert McAlmon, expatriate writer and publisher. His Contact Publishing Company published EH's *Three Stories & Ten Poems*.
Title—*Bird*: William Bird, owner of Three Mountains Press, which published *in our time*.
5—*yence*: To have sexual intercourse.
14—*Bill*: Bill Smith, EH's Chicago friend.
26—*Menken*: Probably S. Stanwood Menken, a reformer; but possibly a misspelling of H. L. Mencken's name. EH later ironically dedicated *The Torrents of Spring* to both of these men "in admiration."
27—*Waldo Frank*: American author of *Virgin Spain* (1926), a book that EH claimed was written in a style of "unavoidable mysticism of a man who writes a language so badly he cannot make a clear statement" (*Death in the Afternoon*, p. 53).
28—*The Broom*: Literary magazine edited by Harold Loeb.
29—*Dada*: Presurrealist school of art and philosophy founded by Tristan Tzara.
30—*Dempsey*: Heavyweight champion Jack Dempsey.
32—*Ezra*: Ezra Pound, EH's friend and mentor. Using Pound's own style of satire, EH offered a celebration of his friend.
46—*The Dial does a monument to Proust*: EH is satirizing the *Dial*'s special issue in honor of Marcel Proust, who had died in November 1922. EH uses this crude satire to promote his belief that, while albeit deserving (but dead) writers like Proust are praised, Ezra Pound does not receive the attention he deserves—especially from the *Dial*. For

more of EH's experiences with the *Dial* see "The Man Who Was Marked for Death," in *A Moveable Feast*, pp. 123-129.

58. Part Two of the Soul of Spain with McAlmon and Bird the Publishers

1—*Veronica*: In bullfighting, receiving the pass of the bull with the cape extended between both hands.

23—*Estocada*: "sword thrust or estocade in which the matador goes in from the front to attempt to place the sword high up between the bull's shoulder blades" (Glossary, *Death in the Afternoon*).

26—*banderillos* (Hemingway apparently meant "banderillas"): "a rounded dowel . . . wrapped in colored paper, with a harpoon shaped steel point, placed in pairs in the withers of the bull in the second act of the bullfight . . ." (Glossary, *Death in the Afternoon*). Banderilleros are the bullfighters who place the banderillas.

28—*diestro*: "skillful; generic term for the Matador" (Glossary, *Death in the Afternoon*).

28—*espada*: "synonym for the sword; also used to refer to the matador himself" (Glossary, *Death in the Afternoon*).

32—*puntillo* (Hemingway apparently meant "puntilla"): "dagger used to kill bull or horse after he has been mortally wounded" (Glossary, *Death in the Afternoon*).

59. To Chink Whose Trade Is Soldiering

Title—*Chink*: EH's lifelong friend Eric Edward Dorman-Smith to whom *in our time* is dedicated.

10—*piste*: Trail (Italian).

60. [Some day when you are picked up . . .]

Undoubtedly, "When you are picked up" is addressed to Eric Edward [Chink] Dorman-Smith, and this poem bears some resemblance to "To Chink Whose Trade Is Soldiering." Since the manuscripts are written in slightly different handwriting styles and on different kinds of paper, it must be assumed that they are separate works.

5—*Ney*: Marshall Ney, the French hero who led his battered troops in the rear guard action during Napoleon's retreat from Russia. His statue stands across from the Closerie des Lilas, one of EH's favorite cafes.

19—*Suizo*: Hotel Suizo, San Sebastian.

25—*Mick Collins*: Irish revolutionary leader and head of state. In 1922, he was assassinated during the civil strife.

26—*Griffith*: Arthur Griffith, who along with Collins, was the leading force in establishing the Irish Free State and was also the first president of the Irish Republic. He died ten days before Collins's assassination.

26—*Chicherin*: George Chicherin. See notes to "They All Made Peace— What Is Peace?" (poem 52).

61. The Lady Poets With Foot Notes

The six lady poets have been identified by Nicholas Joost, in *Ernest Hemingway and the Little Magazines: The Paris Years*, p. 138, as Edna St. Vincent Millay, Alice Kilmer, Sara Teasdale, Zoë Akins, Lola Ridge, and Amy Lowell.

1—*Vanity Fair*: Fashionable New York magazine of the 1920s.

6—*Bill Reedy*: William Marion Reedy, publisher of the St. Louis *Mirror*. Zoë Akins's and Sara Teasdale's poems appeared in his magazine.

10-11—*leading editorial writer N.Y. Tribune*: Burton Rascoe, who ignored EH's expatriate books (see Introduction).

62. The Poem Is By Maera

This poem was written in 1925, during the summer visit to Pamplona that became the subject of *The Sun Also Rises*. EH had been commissioned to work on an illustrated book about bullfighting by Alfred Flechtheim of *Der Querschnitt*. EH probably saw the photograph mentioned in this poem among those in Juanito Quintana's extensive collection. See Baker, *Hemingway Life*, p. 148.

Title—*Maera*: The banderillero and matador, Manuel Garcia. See notes to "To A Tragic Poetess" (poem 67) and *Death in the Afternoon*, pp. 77-83.

1—*Juanito Quintana*: Aficionado and a longtime friend of EH's. He was the owner of the Hotel Quintana in Pamplona; he is fictionalized in *The Sun Also Rises* as Montoya.

1—*Miuras*: A breed of bulls.

2—*Rodolfo Gaona*: A matador known for his cape work. Late in his career, personal problems affected his performance in the ring—which accounts for the tone of this poem.

2—*Jose Gomez*: The bullfighter known as Joselito or Gallito. EH considers his life and death in several passages in *Death in the Afternoon*.

2-3—*Juan Belmonte*: The bullfighter against whom EH judged all other bullfighters.

3—*Banderilleros*: "bullfighter under the orders of the matador and paid by him, who helps run the bull with the cape and places banderillas . . ." (Glossary, *Death in the Afternoon*).

3—*Magritas*: A famous banderillero of the late 1920s and early 1930s.

3—*Almendro*: Joselito's favorite banderillero.

4—*paseo*: "entry of the bullfighters into the ring and their passage across it" (Glossary, *Death in the Afternoon*).

7—*Everybody steps*: Reference to the slow marching steps the matadors take during the paseo, the beginning of the ceremonies.

A Valentine and Other Offerings   1926-1935

63. Neothomist Poem

At one stage, this was a ten-line poem. Ezra Pound, who edited the *Exile*, may have been responsible for turning the poem into an epigram. The last eight lines read more like a dying echo of the Twenty-third Psalm than a parody of it:

> The Lord is my shepherd
>   I shall not want him for long
> He maketh me to lie down in green pastures
>   and there are no green pastures
> He leadeth me beside still waters
>   and still waters run deep
> the wind blows and the bark of the trees is wet from the rain
> the leaves fall and the trees are bare in the wind
> Leaves float on the still waters
> There are wet dead leaves in the basin of the fountain

In a letter to Louis Henry Cohn, EH glossed "neothomist" as "the temporary embracing of the church by literary gents." The literary gent in question in this case was Jean Cocteau, who had moved from opium to religion (Baker, *Hemingway Life*, p. 596). The "thom" in the title may have been meant to suggest Thomas Stearns Eliot. Title—*Neothomist*: Misspelled as "Noethómist" in the *Exile* (an issue pockmarked with typographical errors).

64. [And everything the author knows . . .]

In Paris, EH did most of his writing in notebooks. The pages of these books contain attempts at writing "true sentences," sketches, doodling, fiction, and odd verse such as this piece. The rambling nature of some of these entries suggests that EH wrote much of his poetry as warm-up exercises, early in the morning when he was trying to get the "juice" flowing.

17—*Another author loves his mother*: Probably a reference to D. H. Lawrence and *Sons and Lovers* (1913).

19—*And make much money to drink*: Possibly a reference to F. Scott Fitzgerald, whom EH had met in 1925.

65. [I think that I have never trod . . .]

Title—A parody of Joyce Kilmer's "Trees."

66. [Little drops of grain alcohol . . .]

5—*Mrs. Parker*: Dorothy Parker.

5—*Algonquin*: The Algonquin Hotel, New York, a gathering place for Manhattan wits.

6—*Robinson*: Dorothy Parker's dachshund.

12—*Mr. McGregor*: Robert Benchley's secretary.

12—*Mr. Benchley*: Humorist Robert Benchley.

67. To a Tragic Poetess

There are several accounts of EH reading a very cutting poem about Dorothy Parker at a party hosted by the Archibald MacLeishes in October 1926. This caused a break between EH and Donald Ogden Stewart, and the rest of the guests did not think the poem was very funny either. Indeed, "To a Tragic Poetess" is not funny, and undoubtedly this was the poem EH read that night. The estrangement between EH and Parker was the result of her failure to return the typewriter she had borrowed from him. However, there is no reference to this episode in any version of this poem.

The poem was inspired by Dorothy Parker's first visit to Europe in the summer of 1926. EH saw her often during that year, first in New York and later in Paris. When EH sailed from New York aboard the *Roosevelt* in 1926, Parker, Robert Benchley, and Seward Collins accompanied him so that they might see a little of the Paris Bohemian life for themselves. This group joined with the Gerald Murphys, the Archibald MacLeishes, the F. Scott Fitzgeralds, and the Gilbert Seldeses on the Riviera.

4—*slit both thy wrists*: A reference to one of Dorothy Parker's suicide attempts.

6—*over-veronaled*: Veronal (sodium barbital) is a hypnotic drug. The term means to take an overdose. Seldom used now, veronal was a popular sleeping drug during the early decades of this century, and it was commonly used for suicide attempts. See also Dorothy Parker's poem on suicide, "Résumé."

8—*that undistant country*: In "Poem to Mary" (second poem) EH repeats these lines, but changes "undistant" to "undiscovered." This is a variation on Shakespeare's lines:

> But that the dread of something after death,—
> The undiscovered country, from whose bourn
> No traveller returns,—puzzles the will,
>
>   (*Hamlet*, III, i)

12—*his little hands*: A formed fetus. In one of the early manuscript versions the subtitle contains the ironical phrase "including lines in praise of abortion." See note on 1. 36.

21—*the Seldes*: Gilbert Seldes, managing editor of the *Dial*, and his wife (see Introduction).

22—*One Jew . . . a consumptive*: Probably the Seldeses and Dorothy Parker.

23—*you sneered your way around*: Dorothy Parker's trips to Europe seemed to be mere forays away from New York, though never away from New Yorkers. This inability to enter into the mood and context of a country and its people always angered EH.

31—*Luticia*: A Paris hotel.

36—*Charley*: Charles MacArthur. At the end of her stormy affair with MacArthur, Dorothy Parker became pregnant and had an abortion. This complicated her already frenetic emotional life and shortly thereafter she attempted suicide by slashing her wrists. In two typescripts the ex-lover is named Henry.

44—*Litri*: The "ring" name for Manuel Baez, a young matador who was gored at Malaga in February 1926.

45—*death's other kingdom*: EH borrowed this phrase from T. S. Eliot's *The Hollow Men*:

> Those who have crossed
> With direct eyes, to death's other Kingdom

49—*crise of desespoir*: Crisis of despair (French).

50—*desesperado*: The desperate one (Spanish).

54—*Maera*: Manuel Garcia, Maera, one of the greatest banderilleros and matadors. See notes to "The Poem Is By Maera" (poem 62).

55—*Although Maera slipped from bed*: Maera continued to fight in the bullring until tuberculosis overwhelmed him.

64—*Valentin Magarza*: EH later dramatized this anecdote, with the conclusion characteristically omitted, in the story "A Clean, Well-Lighted Place."

68. Portrait of a Lady

This parody with rhyming couplet is excerpted from a five-page unpublished essay on Gertrude Stein, probably written in Paris about 1926. That would place it at about the time EH's close relationship with Stein came to an end.

Title—The title of a novel by Henry James and a poem by T. S. Eliot. For "Sequel" EH used Eliot's poem once again.

6—*the Sitwells*: Dame Edith Sitwell and her brothers, Osbert and Sacheverell. This upper-class literary family was the subject of much controversy during the 1920s.

69. Sequel

Title—This sequel resembles the opening lines of the last stanza from T. S. Eliot's "Portrait of a Lady":

> Well! and what if she should die some afternoon,
> Afternoon grey and smoky, evening yellow and rose;
> Should die and leave me sitting pen in hand

EH never revised this fragment. It was written about the time he left Hadley.

70. [The rail ends do not meet . . .]

5—*Levine*: Charles Levine flew the Atlantic with Clarence Chamberlin in 1927.

71. Valentine

Subtitle—*Lee Wilson Dodd*: The literary critic whose article "Simple Annals of the Callous," a review of *Men Without Women*, was published in the 19 November 1927 issue of the *Saturday Review of Literature*. "Valentine" was EH's point-blank response. It served as EH's "non-literary" contribution to the last issue of the *Little Review*. For the magazine's final number, Margaret Anderson solicited material that was "not literature" from many avant-garde writers of the age. She published the following letter from Hemingway about "Valentine":

> Enclosed please find a piece for the Final Number of yr. esteemed weekly.
> I hope this will meet with your qualifications that it should not be literature.
> I have been working on this day and night since your letter came and wd. greatly enjoy your acknowleging receipt of same and whether you will use same as there is a great demand for my work by the Atlantic Monthly and kindred periodicals and wd. not like to disappoint these editors when I have a piece so immenently or emminently saleable.
>
> > Yrs. always,
> > HEM

12-16—*(All are very much . . . without a gallus)*: In parentheses EH lists some of the comments that Dodd and others had made about his books.

16—*gallus*: Cock (Latin). Reference to Jake Barnes's wound in *The Sun Also Rises*.

19—*asses*: Margaret Anderson replaced this word with ellipses.

72. Poem, 1928

The poem was written on stationery from the Hotel Bristol, Berlin. In 1929, EH and William Bird had attended the bicycle races there. The text of this poem is conflated from two manuscripts. The first eighteen lines are from what appears to be a new version of the opening of the poem.

1—*They say it's over*: When EH wrote this poem in Berlin in 1929, the critical perspectives in the United States had shifted. The philosophy of experience of the 1920s was repudiated by humanist critics.

18—*bodkins*: Daggers.

73. [Little Mr. Wilson . . .]

In November 1930, EH was in the hospital in Billings, Montana, with a broken right arm. Edmund Wilson's novel, *I Thought of Daisy* (1929), came under his scrutiny, and he was angered by Wilson's introduction to the new 1930 edition of *In Our Time* (Baker, *Hemingway Life*, p. 602). Left-handed, he scribbled the caustic "Little Mr. Wilson . . ." on the back of an x-ray department form.

3—*Maxie Perkins*: Maxwell Perkins, Wilson's and EH's editor at Scribners.

4—*Mr. Snook*: Earl Snook, who visited EH at the hospital.

74. Advice to a Son

Title—Originally titled "Advice to My Son," the poem was written in Germany in September 1931.

75. Lines to Be Read at the Casting of Scott FitzGerald's Balls into the Sea from Eden Roc (Antibes, Alpes Maritimes)

Hemingway wrote to F. Scott Fitzgerald on 21 December 1935, commenting on Fitzgerald's depression:

If you really feel blue enough get yourself heavily insured
and I'll see you can get killed. All you'll have to do is not
put your hands up quick enough and some nigger son of a
bitch will shoot you and your family will be provided for
and you won't have to write anymore, and I'll write you a
fine obituary that Malcolm Cowley will cut the best part out
of for the new republic and we can take your liver out and
give it to the Princeton Museum, your heart to the Plaza
Hotel, and one lung to Max Perkins and the other to
George Horace Lorimer. If we can still find your balls I will
take them via the Ile de France to Paris and down to
Antibes and have them cast into the sea off Eden Roc and
we will get MacLeish to write a Mystic Poem to be read at
that Catholic School (Newman?) you went to. Would you
like me to write the mystic poem now. Let' see.

Title—Possibly a reference to the myth of Aphrodite's birth: Cronus
cut off the testicles of Uranus and threw them into the sea;
Aphrodite sprang from the testicles.
11—*unbenfinneyed*: Ben Finney, a mutual friend of Fitzgerald's and
Hemingway's on the Riviera in the 1920s.

Farewells 1944-1956

76. First Poem to Mary in London

Title—*Mary*: Mary Welsh was a London correspondent for *Time*
when she met EH in 1944. EH wrote this poem for her in May 1944,
while he was in London, staying at the Dorchester Hotel.
8—*a new city*: London. The city was new for EH; none of his
memories were there.
9—*Shy from too long on the water*: EH had gone to the European
theater of the war after pursuing a private war against German
submarines in the Caribbean Sea and the Gulf of Mexico. When EH
went to England to cover the war for *Collier's* and began flying
missions with the Royal Air Force, he felt that he was out of his
element. The loneliness and strangeness that he felt are reflected by
the introverted style and melancholy quality of this poem.

17-18—*my true headache*: The headache that EH refers to was the result of an injury that he had received in an automobile accident a few weeks before writing this poem.

43—*Wolfie*: Winston Guest, who shared the expenses of outfitting the *Pilar* for sub-hunting; he was the model for Henry Wood in *Islands in the Stream*.

43—*Paxtchi*: Francisco Paxtchi Ibarlucea, a Basque mate aboard the *Pilar*.

65—*she will come*: Mary Welsh.

77. Poem to Mary (Second Poem)

EH began "Poem to Mary (Second Poem)" while he was with Colonel Charles (Buck) Lanham and the Twenty-second Infantry Regiment at the Battle of Huertgen Forest and finished it at the Ritz Hotel in Paris in September 1944. EH attached a literary value to this work, beyond its personal value. In *How It Was*, Mary Welsh Hemingway recounts how she was the typist for this poem addressed to her; in a thoughtless moment, she threw away the manuscript after she had finished typing it (pp. 120-121).

There are several dates referred to in the poem which help to fix the period of composition. Dates are given in relationship to D-Day (6 June 1944) and Christmas. Besides the dates for battle (l. 22), EH gives the following dates as "now" in the poem:

132—*D plus 108*: 22 September 1944;

196—*89 more days until Christmas*: 27 September;

205—*D plus one O one O nine*: 23 September;

207—*Christmas minus ninety-nine* (changed to "eighty-nine" in the *Atlantic*): 17 September.

In the only surviving manuscript, *D plus 106*, 20 September, is mentioned as a date of composition.

37—*Archbishop Spellman*: Francis Spellman of New York, who visited the European battlefields.

38—*Air Reduction*: Company that produces various gasses—including inflating gasses.

88-90—*from that undiscovered country . . . who hasn't been there*: (Hamlet, III, i) See notes to "To a Tragic Poetess" (poem 67).

215-227—*So, Mary . . . that I love you*: This closing passage was not published in the *Atlantic*, although it is included in the Caedmon recording of EH reading this poem.

78. Poetry

In *How It Was* (p. 125) Mary Welsh Hemingway quotes from a disturbing letter she received from EH (24 September 1944). "Can't write poetry from too much talking," he wrote, "it started coming out as chickenshit Hiawatha." This fragment was all he could send that day.

79. Defense of Luxembourg

This World War II poem reflects EH's thoughts during the moments that preceded a battle. EH wrote it in 1945, after he had returned to his home in Cuba.
18—*the Scribe*: Paris hotel on the Rue Scribe where the press corps gathered.
45-48—*White . . . S.6 . . . Blue*: Code names for the different groups involved in the attack.
46—*M.G.*: Machine gun.

80. To Crazy Christian

Title—EH's relationship with cats is well-known. He celebrated F. Puss in *A Moveable Feast* and Boise in *Islands in the Stream*. Crazy Christian was one of his favorites, and this poem was written on the day the cat was killed by other cats at the Finca Vigía. That date was never recorded; Mrs. Hemingway remembers it to have been about 1946.

81. Poem to Miss Mary

This poem was written on 20 December 1949. EH wrote six poems in Paris during November and December of 1949, while he and Mary Hemingway were staying at the Ritz Hotel. (The other poems were "Across the Board," "Black-Ass Poem After Talking to Pamela Churchill," "The Road to Avallon," "Country Poem with Little Country" and "Travel Poem.")

82. Across the Board

Title—This poem was composed on a paper napkin in the clubhouse at Paris's Auteuil racetrack. EH used the horseracing metaphor to convey his nostalgic thoughts after meeting one of the French irregulars who had been with him during World War II. See A. E. Hotchner, *Papa Hemingway: A Personal Memoir*, pp. 40-42.
3—*Richard*: EH's wartime aide. Seeing this man reminded EH of those who did not survive the war.

83. Black-Ass Poem After Talking to Pamela Churchill

Title—*Black-Ass*: EH's term for melancholia.
Title—*Pamela Churchill*: Was then the wife of Randolph Churchill. She and Mary Welsh had been acquaintances in London during World War II. The Hemingways ran into her at the Ritz; afterwards, EH retired to his room and wrote this poem.

84. The Road to Avallon

Title—*Avallon*: A town in Yonne, 200 kilometers southeast of Paris. The Hemingways were still in Paris when EH wrote the poem. Avalon may have been on EH's mind, too. It is the island sanctuary where King Arthur was taken after he had been mortally wounded.

85. Country Poem with Little Country

13—*on the line*: The radio frequency between bombers.

87. Lines to a Girl 5 Days After Her 21st Birthday

1-12—*Back To The Palace . . . Who travels alone*: The refrain and the message of the poem were borrowed from Kipling's "Winners":

> Werefore the more ye be holpen and stayed,
> Stayed by a friend in the hour of toil,
> Sing the heretical song I have made—
> His be the labour and yours be the spoil,
> Win by his aid and the aid disown—
> He travels the fastest who travels alone!

1—*The Palace*: The Gritti Palace Hotel, Venice.
3—*She*: The "girl" of the title is Adriana Ivancich, the beautiful

young woman whom EH had befriended in Venice in 1948. In December 1950, Adriana celebrated her twenty-first birthday at Finca Vigia while visiting with her mother.

14—*Harry's Bar*: EH's favorite Venice bar. Some of the scenes of *Across the River and Into the Trees* are set there.

15—*Afderas*: Afdera Franchetti. Adriana's young friend had told the gossip columnists at *Europeo* magazine that she and Adriana were the models for Renata of *Across the River and Into the Trees*, but Afdera went on to claim that she had had an affair with EH— meeting him in Paris and at the Finca Vigia. This "affair" was a complete fiction. See Baker, *Hemingway*, p. 486; and Mary Welsh Hemingway, *How It Was*, p. 273.

The Caedmon recording of *Ernest Hemingway Reading* (1965) contains an extemporaneous parody of *Across the River and Into the Trees*. The hero of "In Harry's Bar in Venice" is an eighteen-year-old colonel who is in love with an eighty-six-year-old Venetian countess. He finally falls for a Venetian maiden, one Afdera. She is "indomitable—nothing like her has been seen since Attila the Hun. . . . Afdera loves him as she loves the front page of *Europeo*."

15—*Lido*: An island and the exclusive beachfront area of Venice.

16—*Translator's note*: EH's.

18—*Mondadori*: EH's Italian publisher.

22—*Wake up in the mornings*: At this point, the poem becomes a dialogue between EH and Adriana. This is not a love poem, but rather an exchange between artists, one old and one young. EH's revision of Kipling's refrain to "She travels the fastest / Who travels alone" is both a statement of her destiny, if she can make the proper sacrifices, and a recognition of the solitude that can defeat her. He will not stand in the way of the young artist, but he knows there is nothing he can do to help. Adriana may only be talented in the way "Everyone is talented at a certain age"—which was Renata's epitaph for her own gift.

88. [If my Valentine you won't be . . .]

Mary Welsh Hemingway quotes this Valentine's Day couplet that EH wrote for her in 1956 (*How It Was*, p. 428). EH had grown so fond of their Christmas tree that he would not allow it to be removed until months after Christmas.

Critical Intelligence

Your mother is not my mother
is not
my mother
is not beautiful
your father is not my father
is not
my father
is not wonderful
you go at night where I go at night
but we do not go together
one and one makes three
to work if possible
with no loss of amusement
night becomes no different
prayers cannot always be said
nor are letters always received in the morning
letters are written on the typewriter
fortunately the furnace remains lighted
night is the same as day as dull as happy
there are no night changes
one hour is as good as another all of the twenty four were
received from the Lord in a sealed package and on being opened
contained breakfast food
And for what did we what did we what did they
give us what?
They cancelled our tickets
there are no more unknown countries to come to the bed at
night in the dark it is all the same now as in daylight
fortunately your family your father your mother your sister
not your brother unless I say not your brother also exciting
dreams
where I am not
there nor anywhere but in the bed beside you
perhaps you still go places in the night the night can be so
lovely in the night in the dark
it is not a question of loving I love you more than love you and
you love me but where do you go then and why must you
go and what

if there is no difference really and night the same as day
then what was the why was the what was the
certainly I understand you what you say is very simple and easy
to answer let me put it to you very simply
what was the what was the
yes it is very simple and clear the answer is perfectly obvious
there is nothing far fetched about it nor any unreasonable
difficulty you demand to know
what was the what was the what was the what
absolutely I hope that is clear we can now I hope consider
the matter closed as always there are no difficulties if the
what was the what was the what was the what was the what was the
    what
I think we have finished with that question and the literature of
the future I might inform you in passing will be written
by bland young gentlemen of whom at this time absolutely nothing
is known.
Thank You.

Paris, ca. 1927

Afterword to the Revised Edition

When I completed the original edition of Hemingway's collected poems twelve years ago, I expected to be frustrated and embarrassed before the ink had dried by the discovery of a new trunk of unpublished material. At the very least, I thought the authorized edition would inspire the private collectors to reveal their holdings. But then I am one who cannot imagine that Lord Elgin never doubted his actions while he was cleaning out the Parthenon.

Since 1980, when the Hemingway Room was officially dedicated at the John F. Kennedy Library, ever more Hemingway material has steadily found its way to the library, where the staff has patiently cataloged it. It has been like a great family reunion; Hemingway's wayward manuscripts, letters, scraps, and snapshots coming together to be recognized after years of living in obscurity. And many outsiders have cared. Biographies of Hemingway seem to battle each other for space on the book stands. The library of new material at the Kennedy has been quoted and printed in books and journal articles. New material seems to give credibility to the critic's interpretation of a life. Some of the new writing on Hemingway is good and true. The best is by Michael Reynolds. In his multivolume life of Hemingway, Reynolds is getting the facts right, and his instincts for his subject are right, too.

The new biographers are quoting from the poems; I especially notice references to those poems that had appeared for the first time in the authorized edition. So, in a small way, the poems have made their marks. I have also been intrigued by the interest in the poems by editors of poetry anthologies. The poems have not been given too much credit; they have simply taken their place as curious, personal footnotes to a life that remains elusive. The best critical comments on the poems remain those of Linda Wagner in "Hemingway as Poet," her appendix to *Hemingway and Faulkner: Inventors/Masters*, a work that I was unfamiliar with when I wrote the notes for the first edition. Another important critical study of Hemingway's work that I neglected to mention in the gloss to the first edition is Colin Wilson's remarkable book of literary philosophy, *The Outsiders*; Wilson's chapter on Hemingway is exciting, and it inspired me while I was writing my philosophical survey, "Hemingway's Poetry: Angry Notes of an Ambivalent Overman."

Critical intelligence on the poems has grown modestly, but "new" poems have not been plentiful. In his biographical accompaniment to some of Hemingway's previously unpublished works, *Along with Youth*, Peter Griffin published "The Day," a piece of juvenilia that he identifies as belonging to Hemingway. The work is not included in the collection at the Kennedy Library; since it is available for the general reader in Griffin's book, I have elected not to include it in this revised edition. Furthermore, some of the biographers have referred to a poem that I identified in my original introduction (cf. 2, xxv). A few words need to be said here about the controversial "Hurray for Fonnie Richardson." It is reactionary in sentiment and includes racist language; it is bluntly the words of a brother-in-law who is repulsively angry at his sister-in-law. The doggerel verse has been paraphrased and danced around by biographers and critics; apparently it is about to be published in a new biography of Hadley Richardson. The poem is an attack on Fonnie, Hadley's sister. Unlike the poems in this collection, it has no public purpose to its composition. Quite simply, I could never convince anyone that Hemingway would have ever intended to allow this poem to be put in print. I repeat here that my charge from Mary Hemingway was not to publish anything that would hurt a living person. Hadley was alive when the first edition was published. Now she and Mary are dead. But I still believe that "Hurray for Fonnie Richardson" could hurt a living person. I am not going to publish it.

Nor am I ready to attempt to publish the other controversial poems identified in the original introduction. So, within these boundaries, the works contained here constitute the complete poems. Originally, I simply entitled them by their number; I never expected them to be all there was, and I still do not.

Thanks to Mike Reynolds, I became aware of "Critical Intelligence," published here for the first time. I am very pleased to be able to include this work, which I believe was composed during a poignant time in Hemingway's life. In October 1927, *Men without Women* was published and greeted by tough reviews. "Valentine" is a poetic reaction to that criticism. However, "Critical Intelligence," although it reflects Hemingway's consciousness of some of the more stinging statements in those reviews, is mostly a nocturnal experiment with language inspired by the return to Paris of Hadley Hemingway. Hadley and Ernest were divorced. Ernest was now married to Pauline. When Hadley had departed for the United States some months before, she had been distraught and overweight. In October 1927, she returned to Paris healthy, beautiful, and in control. "Critical Intelligence" is a disturbing poem; its echos of Hadley's lingering effect on Ernest can be found in everything from "The Snows of Kilimanjaro" through *A Moveable Feast, Islands in the Stream,* and *Garden of Eden* (especially in the great unpublished portions of that unfortunate novel).

"Critical Intelligence" exists in a manuscript first version and a typescript revision (items #342, 343, 406, and 407 in the Kennedy Library's catalog of Hemingway manuscripts). The Kennedy's numbering sequences for the drafts indicates that the archivists are treating the documents as separate works, because the pages probably did not surface together. It is my opinion that the material beginning with line 29 ("fortunately your family . . .") makes up the second page of the typescript titled "Critical Intelligence" (Kennedy, items #406 and 407). The typescript is by Hemingway; the telltale signs of accidental spacing (possibly anxious fingers, or a slipping typewriter carriage) and spaced punctuation placement are uniquely his. The typescript is significantly different from the manuscript; as has been my method, I have used the author's last apparent version as the copytext for publication. I have emended the typescript in three places, using Hemingway's manuscript to correct what I believe are accidental errors. The first line in the typescript is one space further left than all of the other lines of the poem. I believe this was the result of a problem with the carriage (a forceful return?); the manuscript does not indicate an intention on Hemingway's part to use indentation here, or elsewhere, in this poem for stylistic purposes. So I have made all of the lines flush left. The lower portion of the first page of the typescript is damaged and difficult to read; I have referred to the typescript to complete lines 24-25 ("And for what . . . give us what?"). I believe this reading was Hemingway's intent in this passage. Finally, I corrected an obvious typographical error in line 44 of the typescript ("nor" for "no") in order to conform to the manuscript.

The manuscript version, revised by Hemingway in the typescript, is interesting. For example, there is an *envoi* at the beginning of the poem in the manuscript preceding the opening lines that reads:

A little poem because I love you a big poem
to make you proud a small poem not
to be comfortable neither now nor then
or now nor forever

(Neither now nor then
or now nor forever
one and one make three
because I love you
nor does the furnace heat
nor does my heart beat)

This *envoi* is for Hadley, but I do not know whether she ever saw it or any version of "Critical Intelligence." When I spoke with her and communicated with her by letter in the late 1970s, she never referred to this poem. Of course, she could have forgotten about it. The poem is addressed to Hadley; the references are to the Richardson family: Florence Richardson, her mother; James Richardson, Jr., her father, dead by suicide when she was fourteen; sister Fonnie, and brother James. If she had seen this poem, Hadley would have recognized the strange nocturnal quality of some of Ernest's earlier poems that he had sent to her when she was still living in St. Louis and he was working in Chicago. And she probably would have smiled at the familiar stylistic influence of Gertrude Stein, the godmother of their young son. Perhaps what would not have been as clear to her are the references in the last five lines of the poem ("the literature of the future . . . will be written by bland young gentlemen") that are echos of the reviewers' comments on *Men without Women*. He was sharing his literary battles with her, as he was accustomed to doing. But she was no longer his wife. It was just a little touch of Ernest in the night. The sadness anticipates the style of the poems Ernest wrote to Mary in the 1940s.

As important as it is to me to add this poem to the collection through this revised edition, it is also important to me to be able to correct some of the mistakes I made in the first edition. Some errors have been corrected in the text (where new typesetting has not posed a problem). There are a few matters that need more space.

First of all, my apologies to Hugh Ford, whose work has been a joy for everyone interested in the Paris scene between the wars. Of course Gertrude Stein's short review of Hemingway's *Three Stories and Ten Poems* (p. xv) was published in the *Chicago Tribune* European Edition (27 November 1923), and Professor Ford has reprinted it in his excellent collection *The Left Bank Revisited* (p. 257). I simply missed it.

My note on "D'Annunzio" (p. 135) is woefully incomplete. Following the publication of the first edition of the poems, I pursued my interest in Hemingway's persistent references to this strange Italian, perhaps Europe's last man of the nineteenth century. I delivered my findings during the dedication of the Hemingway Room at the Kennedy in 1980. For the interested reader, "Hemingway's Poems: Angry Notes of an Ambivalent Overman" can be found in *Ernest Hemingway: The Papers of a Writer* and in *Ernest Hemingway: Six Decades of Criticism*.

Hemingway's epigram to "To a Tragic Poetess" (p. 87)— "Nothing in her life became her like her almost leaving of it."— captures the essence of this attack on Dorothy Parker. Of course the point of this lance is the word *almost*. Hemingway was alluding to Shakespeare's lines:

> . . . nothing in his life
> Became him like the leaving of it; he died
> As one that had been studied in his death
> To throw away the dearest thing he owed,
> As 'twere a careless trifle.
>
> (*Macbeth*, I, iv)

The lines are spoken by Malcolm, upon the execution of the traitor Cawdor.

I have done the best I could. I am indebted to Michael Reynolds. I want to thank George Whitman, proprietor of Shakespeare and Company, Kilometer zero Paris, for allowing me to read in his private library of expatriate publications, and for the tea. I appreciate the trustworthy archivists at the Kennedy Library; scholars who are interested in the Hemingway manuscripts at the Kennedy should request copies of the catalog and supplement. The Hemingway

Foundation has granted permission for the previously unpublished material to be included. Most of all, I appreciate the efforts of the University of Nebraska Press for initiating the work for this revised edition, and I am indebted to the press for keeping Hemingway's poems in print.

In the summer of 1990, I walked into the Gallimard bookstore on the boulevard Raspail in Paris, where I easily located a copy of the French edition of this book (expertly translated by Roger Asselineau). This experience gave me pleasure: Hemingway's poems, many inspired by his French milieu, in French, in a bookstore on the Left Bank in the city of his education. I believe Hemingway would have been amused, too.

Nicholas Gerogiannis
September 1991

Related Readings

Books by Hemingway

Three Stories & Ten Poems. Paris: Contact Publishing Company, 1923; facsimile reprint Bloomfield Hills, Mich. & Columbia, S.C.: Bruccoli Clark, 1978.

in our time. Paris: Three Mountains Press, 1924; facsimile reprint, Bloomfield Hills, Mich. & Columbia, S.C.: Bruccoli Clark, 1978.

In Our Time: Stories. New York: Boni & Liveright, 1925.

The Torrents of Spring. New York: Scribners, 1926.

The Sun Also Rises. New York: Scribners, 1926.

Men Without Women. New York: Scribners, 1927.

A Farewell to Arms. New York: Scribners, 1929.

Four Poems. Twelve copies privately printed by Louis Henry Cohn, 31 August 1930.

Death in the Afternoon. New York: Scribners, 1932.

The Fifth Column and The First Forty-Nine Stories. New York: Scribners, 1938.

Across the River and Into the Trees. New York: Scribners, 1950.

A Moveable Feast. New York: Scribners, 1964.

By-Line: Ernest Hemingway, ed. William White. New York: Scribners, 1967.

Islands in the Stream. New York: Scribners, 1970.

Ernest Hemingway's Apprenticeship, ed. Matthew J. Bruccoli. Washington, D.C.: Bruccoli Clark / NCR Microcard Editions, 1971.

88 Poems, ed. Nicholas Gerogiannis. New York: Harcourt Brace Jovanovich/Bruccoli Clark, 1979.

Selected Letters 1917–1961, ed. Carlos Baker. New York: Scribners, 1981.

Ernest Hemingway on Writing, ed. Larry W. Phillips. New York: Scribners, 1984.

The Dangerous Summer. New York: Scribners, 1985.

The Garden of Eden. New York: Scribners, 1986.

The Complete Short Stories of Ernest Hemingway, The Finca Vigia Edition. New York: Scribners, 1987.

Books about Hemingway

Baker, Carlos. *Ernest Hemingway: A Life Story*. New York: Scribners, 1969.

Baker. *Hemingway: The Writer as Artist*, fourth edition. Princeton: Princeton University Press, 1972.

Brian, Denis. *The True Gen: An Intimate Portrait of Hemingway by Those Who Knew Him*. New York: Grove Press, 1987.

Bruccoli, Matthew J. *Scott and Ernest*. New York: Random House, 1978.

Fenton, Charles A. *The Apprenticeship of Ernest Hemingway*. New York: Farrar, Straus & Young, 1954.

Ford, Hugh, ed. *The Left Bank Revisited*. State College, Penn.: Pennsylvania State University Press, 1972.

Fuentes, Norberto. *Ernest Hemingway Rediscovered*. New York: Scribners, 1988.

––––––. *Hemingway in Cuba*. Secaucus, N.J.: Lyle Stuart, 1984.

Griffin, Peter. *Along with Youth: Hemingway, the Early Years*. New York: Oxford University Press, 1985.

––––––. *Less Than a Treason: Hemingway in Paris*. New York: Oxford University Press, 1990.

Hanneman, Audre. *Ernest Hemingway: A Comprehensive Bibliography*. Princeton: Princeton University Press, 1967; supplement, 1975.

Hemingway, Mary Welsh. *How It Was*. New York: Knopf, 1976.

Hotchner, A. E. *Papa Hemingway: A Personal Memoir*. New York: Random House, 1966.

Joost, Nicholas. *Ernest Hemingway and the Little Magazines: The Paris Years*. Barre, Mass.: Barre Publishers, 1968.

Meyers, Jeffrey. *Hemingway: A Biography*. New York: Harper and Row, 1985.

Oldsey, Bernard, ed. *Ernest Hemingway: The Papers of a Writer*. New York: Garland, 1981.

Reichard, Daniel P., ed. *Ernest Hemingway in High School: Writings About and By Ernest Hemingway as They Appeared in the Publications of Oak Park and River Forest High School 1916–1919*. Oak Park and River Forest High School, 1969. Microfilm.

Reynolds, Michael. *The Young Hemingway*. New York: Basil Blackwell, 1987.

––––––. *Hemingway: The Paris Years*. New York: Basil Blackwell, 1990.

Young, Philip and Mann, Charles W. *The Hemingway Manuscripts: An*

Inventory. University Park & London: Pennsylvania State University Press, 1969.

Wagner, Linda W., ed. *Ernest Hemingway: Six Decades of Criticism.* East Lansing: Michigan State University Press, 1987.

———. *Hemingway and Faulkner: Inventors/Masters.* Metuchen, N.J.: Scarecrow Press, 1975.

Acknowledgments

All too briefly, I want the thank the following people for their assistance and encouragement: Mary Welsh Hemingway, for permission to publish the poems; Hadley Mowrer, for her permission to use some of her letters to Ernest Hemingway, and Richard Mowrer for his aid; Jo August, Curator of the Hemingway Collection at the John F. Kennedy Library, for her invaluable aid and sense of humor; Matthew J. Bruccoli and Richard Layman, for their editorial guidance; Thomas S. Lawson, Jr., for his assistance and support; Carlos Baker, for his patience and expert suggestions; A. E. Hotchner, for permission to use "Across the Board" and for the anecdote; and Sharon Speer Gerogiannis and K. L. Deal, for hours of proofreading and editing. Burton Wright helped type the manuscript.

Because of conflicting information—and because I have been working with new material—I have used my own judgment in many instances, but I owe special debts to Carlos Baker's *Ernest Hemingway: A Life Story*, Charles A. Fenton's *The Apprenticeship of Ernest Hemingway*, Audre Hanneman's *Ernest Hemingway: A Comprehensive Bibliography*, Philip Young and Charles W. Mann's *The Hemingway Manuscripts*, and Oak Park and River Forest High School's microfilm of Ernest Hemingway's high-school publications. (A more complete list of sources appears under Related Readings.)

The Inter-Library Loan Department of the University of Iowa Libraries found copies of rare magazines, and the Graduate College and Department of English of the University granted me travel funds for my research in New York and Boston.